CHINA

AN INSIDER'S GUIDE:

LETTERS FROM A CHANGING NATION

Published by
Alain Charles Asia Publishing Ltd.
University House
11-13 Lower Grosvenor Place,
London SW1W 0EX, UK
Tel: +44 (0)20 7834 7676 Fax: +44 (0)20 7973 0076
E-mail: info@alaincharlesasia.com
Web: www.alaincharlesasia.com/publications

The greatest care has been taken to ensure accuracy but the
publisher can accept no responsibility for errors or omissions, or
for any liability occasioned by relying on its content.

ISBN: 978-0-9927625-2-0

A catalogue record for China - an Insider's Guide: Letters from
a Changing Nation is available from the National Bibliographic
Service of the British Library.

Introduction

China is impossible to encapsulate. Confronted with its size, history and complexity, commentators too often resort to easy generalisations.

Accordingly, much international media coverage swings from the evangelistic ("China will rule the world") to the apocalyptic ("China's about to collapse").

In contrast, this series of regular letters – published here in book form – presents the real China that we see every day. We hope that these can offset the frequently hysterical media depictions of the country and, gradually and cumulatively, show what life is actually like for China's millions of citizens.

We don't cover specifically investment-related themes; instead, we aim to explore a broad range of the economic, social and cultural issues that concern ordinary Chinese people today.

The letters collected here span the period 2012 to mid-2014. We hope that you find the letters interesting.

The company behind these letters, designed to inform and entertain, is Open Door. Based in Shanghai, Open Door's large and hard-working team of analysts locates what we believe to be China's most promising entrepreneurial companies. We see management ownership as key in aligning company and investors' interests. Local knowledge and a clear understanding of an investment target in the context of its rivals, suppliers and customers, as well as government policy, are vital to reduce risk.

We have an experienced team in San Francisco to handle trading, legal, compliance, marketing and client services. Open Door Capital Advisors (US), LLC and Open Door Investment Management (US), Ltd. are SEC-registered investment advisors.

We are committed to transparency in our investments. We explain to investors exactly what companies we are investing in and why. We encourage investors to visit us in China or San Francisco to better understand how we work. Our door stands open.

OPEN DOOR
Capital Group
開心龍基金管理公司

Disclaimer

The material in this book is for information purposes only, is general in nature, is not intended as specific or individualized investment, legal, or tax advice, and does not constitute and should not be construed as an offering or solicitation of advisory services or products, or a promise to undertake or solicit business.

The authors make no representation or offering of any analysis, report, graph, chart, formula or other device or publication to be used in making any determination as to when to buy or sell any security, nor of any other investment advisory service with regard to securities, and nothing in this book should be construed as a recommendation that you buy, sell or hold any security or other investment or that you pursue any investment style or strategy.

Under no circumstances should any material in this book be used or considered as an offer to sell or a solicitation of any offer to buy an interest in any investment fund managed or advised by Open Door Capital Group or its affiliates. Any such offer or solicitation will be made only by means of a confidential private offering memorandum relating to the particular fund.

Access to information about any fund is limited to investors who either qualify as accredited investors within the meaning of the United States Securities Act of 1933, as amended, qualified purchasers within the meaning of the United States Investment Company Act of 1940, or those investors who generally are sophisticated in financial matters such that they are capable of evaluating the merits and risks of prospective investments.

Readers who would like investment, accounting, tax or legal advice should consult with their own qualified investment professional(s) with respect to their individual circumstances and needs.

Past performance is not indicative of future results; no representation is being made that any investment will or is likely to achieve profits or losses similar to those achieved in the past, or that significant losses will be avoided.

Contents

2014

Chapter 1

The incredible shrinking Bund

In China, wedding photos are a serious business. The home of any couple married in the last few decades inevitably contains a fat album to be displayed to visitors. The shots themselves can feature a startling array of costumes, often with a distinctly nostalgic element. So a Western-style bridal gown paired with top hat and tails might sit alongside a red qipao, Ming or Manchu robes and headdresses, and, in some cases, even more extravagant historical get up: the pomp of ancien regime France, for example.

The photographs aren't taken on the day itself. Indeed, Chinese weddings can be rather perfunctory affairs: the guests turn up, deposit red envelopes containing gifts of cash, and then sit down to dinner. And that, by and large, is it.

The wedding photos often take much longer – sometimes days rather than hours. Affluent couples will hire photographers to shoot them in historic or picturesque areas of their home towns. The exceptionally well-heeled might even take a plane to some exotic location: the tropical beaches of Hainan, for example. Sophisticates can be snobbish about the most obvious choices, preferring the offbeat or obscure. But for most people, well-known locations will do fine. And physical and financial constraints often lead to cut-price solutions: so, while the happy couple change costumes and props in a photographer's studio, the photographer merely switches the digital backdrop. In this way, soon-to-be-weds in a drab suburb of Beijing or Guangzhou can be whisked past a succession of China's iconic locales: the Great Wall, the Forbidden City, the limestone mountains of Guilin, and, representing Shanghai, the Bund.

The Bund, or waitan ("foreign shore"), has been Shanghai's most distinctive feature for almost a century. Shanghai is not the only Chinese city to boast a colonial waterfront – Wuhan has a bund too (the term itself is a Hindi loanword). But it's the Shanghai version that is the Bund. Largely built in the 1920s and 30s, its buildings were home to trading houses, hotels and banks. Many retain the same functions today, although the institutions have changed, while others house bars, restaurants or – inevitably in contemporary China – luxury retailers.

Shanghai may be the most cosmopolitan city in China, but the Bund is one place where the mere sight of foreigners can cause real excitement; not among the native Shanghainese, but among the thousands of domestic tourists who pack the waterfront every day. For some

Something new ... a couple pose in front of the skyscrapers of Shanghai's financial district

of these visitors, genuine laowai are a bonus attraction, especially foreign children – as mine discovered this weekend, when they were snapped by a succession of cheerful provincial visitors. The kids weren't the only portrait subjects, of course. Dotted around the thronging tourists were the inevitable brides-to-be in white dresses or red qipao. "Look at all the princesses," said my three-year-old.

The Bund runs for about a mile along the edge of the Huangpu River, marking the edge of Puxi and facing, across the river, the modern financial centre of Pudong. Chinese placenames often have a pleasing compass-point symmetry: as, for example, in the provincial pairs of Hunan and Hubei (south and north of the lake, respectively), Henan and Hebei (south and north of the river), Shanxi and Shandong (west and east of the mountains), and Guangdong and Guangxi (the eastern and western expanses). And then there are Nanjing and Beijing (the southern and northern capitals). The Huangpu River (or Pujiang) bisects Shanghai, so Pudong and Puxi are "east and west of the (Huang)Pu".

Seen from Zhongshan Road, which winds along the Puxi waterfront, the Bund is undoubtedly impressive. The foursquare colonial buildings dominate the outlook as they have done for almost a century. To maintain that effect, the authorities have banned the erection of tall buildings in the immediate vicinity. Some way off, to the north and south, modern skyscrapers stand at a discreet distance, allowing the Bund to command the western shore.

Opposite, in Pudong, stand the icons of modern Shanghai – most obviously the Oriental Pearl TV Tower, whose concrete tripod, bulbous spheres and spiked steeple have come to symbolise China's largest city almost as much as the Bund (though they are more reminiscent

Now you see it ... in the 1980s, the Bund was the Puxi skyline

of 1950s science fiction than anything else); indeed, Shanghai wedding shots sometimes now include the Pudong panorama as well as (or instead of) the Bund, with the Pearl Tower, the sleek pierced chisel of the World Financial Centre and the elegantly terraced Jinmao Tower.

But it's the view from the Pudong shore – and especially from the towering structures of the financial district – that puts the Bund in its true context. For the infrequent visitor to Shanghai, the Bund – unchanged as it appears from Zhongshan Road – is steadily shrinking. While the view from the Puxi shore preserves the illusion of colonial grandeur, the Pudong view leaves the waterfront buildings much diminished. Although the Puxi high-rises keep a respectful distance, the Pudong perspective reveals the extent to which the Bund is dwarfed by the mass of vast buildings behind it – buildings whose height and number has been increasing relentlessly over the past couple of decades. The Peace Hotel (formerly the Sassoon House) is the tallest building on the

Bund; when it was built in the 1920s, it was the tallest in the city. Today, countless mundane shapes tower over it: apartment buildings, office blocks and shopping malls. Seen from across the Huangpu, the Bund looks little more than a quaint relic.

To Christopher Isherwood, who visited Shanghai in 1938, the Bund was "only a façade"; behind the apparent civilisation of the waterfront lurked crowded alleys, overflowing slums and, at that time, marauding bands of Japanese soldiers. "Nowhere a fine avenue, a spacious park, an imposing central square," Isherwood lamented, " Nowhere anything civic at all."

Today, the Bund is still just a façade. But rather than providing Shanghai

Now you don't ... from Pudong today, the Bund is only just discernible against a backdrop of skyscrapers

with a mask of modernity, it's merely a historical ornament on a surging mega-city – a city now equipped with a multitude of fine avenues, spacious parks, and, just 10 minutes' walk from the Bund, an imposing central square.

And this is perhaps a fitting fate for the Bund: its buildings reduced to mere foothills of the mountainous structures behind. The colonial façade was, after all, closely linked to oppression, bloodshed and horror: see, for example, the Shanghai-born JG Ballard's descriptions of the beheadings, slaughter and nautical warfare before the Bund in his semi-autobiographical Empire of the Sun. There were grim indignities in more peaceful times too. At the northern end of the Bund, the Public Garden was famously off-limits to both dogs and Chinese between 1890 and 1928; its modern incarnation, Huangpu Park, admits all visitors, whether on four legs or two. This, undoubtedly, is progress.

All progress comes at a price, however. Shanghai has undergone astonishing changes since Isherwood and Ballard's time; indeed, its gleaming shopping malls and gated luxury apartment blocks match Ballard's dystopian science fiction rather than his accounts of wartime China. The pace of change can be distressing: some older Shanghainese complain that they can no longer speak Shanghaihua in shops and restaurants; the service staff, almost always immigrants from other provinces, can only communicate with them in Mandarin. As the city sprawls outwards, soaring house prices and rents have forced many residents from the centre to the suburbs, where they face tiresome commutes on the efficient but grossly overcrowded underground trains. And then there is the pollution that so often shrouds the Bund in smog. That said, the city is stabilising. Fifteen years ago, the Shanghai skyline was a forest of cranes. Today, construction continues, but it is much reduced: as I look across the Huangpu today, only a handful of cranes stand out between the skyscrapers in any direction. Most of those cranes have migrated to inland cities, where the likes of Chongqing, Xi'an and Guiyang are undergoing the sort of construction boom that Shanghai has largely completed. Meanwhile entirely new cities are being conjured from the earth to sustain the Chinese government's massive urbanisation programme – which, by 2030, will have moved the equivalent of the entire population of the US from the countryside to the cities.

So Shanghai, with the shrunken colonial façade of Puxi and the sci-fi sheen of Pudong, points the way to the China of the future. It is doubtless a future of greatly enhanced prosperity for millions of Chinese citizens. But at the same time, I wonder if it is a future that will fuel the same yearning for the past – for stone buildings, antique costumes and tradition – that can be detected in the wedding albums of today.

A Letter From China
21 May 2012
Justin Crozier

Chapter 2

Journey to the West

I first went to Chongqing as a child, 25 years ago, when my father was posted there with the army. My memories from that time are of spicy boiled fish, thick fog and endless stone steps.

But the key images from the successive business trips I have made to Chongqing are of the dynamic change taking place in this ancient, hilly city. When I visited the city at the end of February 2012, it was just before the start of the annual National People's Congress in Beijing. Red lanterns hung from trees everywhere, bringing some welcome warmth to early spring. Under Bo Xilai, the populist former party secretary whose spectacular downfall was yet to come, the "mountain city" had become known as "Red Chongqing".

Standing at the confluence of the Jialing and Yangtze rivers, Chongqing is one of just four municipalities directly controlled by the central government (the others are Beijing, Shanghai and Tianjin) and the only one in western China; until 1997, the city was part of Sichuan province. The municipal area, which includes rural counties as well as the city itself, has a population of about 29 million. It is the largest industrial, commercial and communications centre in western China, and the region's biggest inland port. As such, the city is expected to be a key driver of the Chinese economy. Chongqing has also been chosen to pilot comprehensive reforms to improve the integration of urban and rural areas.

Certainly, the city has been making remarkable progress. In 2011, Chongqing achieved year-on-year GDP growth of 16.4%, the highest among all the provincial-level regions of China. In the same year, fixed-asset investment reached Rmb760 billion, up by 30% year on year. Of this, some Rmb201 billion was investment in property, up 24% on the previous year. To facilitate the shift of industry from the east and south of the country to the west, the city government is planning and developing a new district, Liangjiangxing, to cater to the automobile, airplane, electronics, bio-pharm and port-related industries. The authorities have ambitious plans for Liangjiangxing, with its 2020 GDP expected to match the 2010 total for the entire city. This will entail huge capital spending on commodities and machinery. Already, the

construction sites across the city remind me very much of Shanghai 15 years ago.

There are 51 listed companies in Chongqing, with a total market cap of around Rmb300 billion. Asset-securitisation is a key aim of the city's state-owned enterprises. The number of listed companies is expected to increase to around 100 by 2015. There are around 50

smaller companies that have raised the money through the local OTC market, with a total market cap of Rmb7 billion.

At the moment, we have no investments in Chongqing-based companies; the city has more than its fair share of state-owned and heavy industrial stocks, which we tend to avoid.

Urbanisation is a major issue for Chongqing, and the municipal government has been creative in seeking solutions. "Land tickets", a Chongqing innovation, are proving successful here. In line with the nation's requirement to protect 1.8 billion mu of farming land, the Chongqing government re-cultivates idle rural land. Farmers are rewarded with land tickets (one ticket per mu), and land-ticket transactions are made using a bidding system, through the Chongqing Rural Land Exchange. The government, property developers, companies and private individuals can buy land tickets through this platform. In 2011, the land-ticket trade recorded a turnover of 89,000 mu (6,100 hectares), with a transaction value of Rmb17.5 billion. All proceeds are distributed back to the countryside, with

85% going directly to the farmers and 15% put towards construction and upgrades in rural areas. The Chongqing government is also encouraging financing in rural areas, where total loans reached Rmb18 billion last year. This is slated to increase to Rmb100 billion in 2015. More than 3.2 million farmers have already participated in a pilot scheme whereby they can give up their land in return for a city hukou (China's internal passport which qualifies the owner for social benefits). The farmers are given a three-year grace period during which they can change their minds.

Chongqing is the only major Chinese city without purchase restrictions on property, but it is also one of the few cities with a recurring property tax (although this raised only Rmb100 million in 2010). The objectives of the city government are practical: to guarantee low-end availability through construction of affordable housing (it plans to build some 40 million square metres in the next three years to house 2 million people – over 30% of the city's low-income population); to protect the middle (where there is solid demand); and to restrict the high end (through the property tax). This "governing for the people" is very much in line with former president Hu Jintao's "harmonious society" concept. Chongqing claims to be one of the few places in China where the Gini coefficient (a key measure of inequality) has fallen in recent times.

Given its eventful history, Chongqing has a colourful reputation. It was Chiang Kai-shek's war-time capital; when I first visited the city, you could still see the caves where the population sheltered from Japanese bombers. In 2012, it echoed to the singing of revolutionary songs that Bo Xilai had reintroduced (much to the mockery of people outside, but not inside, Chongqing). Meanwhile, the city's traffic policewomen have been officially recognized as the prettiest in China.

But what's most striking about Chongqing is the creative way in which its administrators are managing its rapid economic growth. The city is leading the development of western China – which we believe will offset the slowdown in other parts of the country. The retro red anthems may not have outlasted Bo Xilai, but the city's rapid progress is here to stay.

A Letter From Chongqing
22 March 2012
Rebecca Yang

Chapter 3

China in microcosm

Ningxia is one of China's smallest and poorest provinces. In terms of GDP, it outranks only Qinghai and Tibet. Just 6 million people live here, of which one-third belong to the Muslim Hui minority. This is probably the reason why, in 30 years of travelling around China, Ningxia is one of only two provinces I never visited. Now only Hainan remains. One might think that such a peripheral province has little to tell us about where China is heading. I found, to the contrary, that many of the key developments and challenges in China are here being played out in miniature.

After arriving at night at the provincial capital, Yinchuan, after a three-hour flight from Shanghai, there was little to be seen. Yinchuan, like most of China, is poorly lit. But when I threw open the bedroom curtains at my hotel (the Kempinski – the first smart hotel in Yinchuan) the view was impressive. In the distance were the high and jagged Helan mountains, which are all that separate Ningxia from the Gobi desert, still showing traces of snow on the peaks. In the near distance was the new town, with broad boulevards and an impressive quantity of parks and lakes. It is clear that a large amount of money has been spent here on "greening" and public amenities. There was, of course, a smart new local Communist Party headquarters, built to the same monumentalist design employed in most of China's large cities. But there was also an array of impressive new public buildings – museums, a stadium, new university buildings, an exhibition centre – into which a deal of architectural thought had clearly gone. The local party chiefs have recently been given "cultural" targets as well as economic ones, to which they have responded by building many such edifices. They might not be quite sure about "culture", but they know cement very well (and cement pays better). The next challenge (to be left to future cadres) will be how to fill them.

Generally, I found the infrastructure in Ningxia good. The road system is excellent. My car ran on natural gas, along with around half the cars in Yinchuan, according to the driver. My mobile phone worked even in remote countryside. None of the companies I met complained of any shortage of power or water. If cranes have disappeared from the Shanghai skyline, it may be because they have all come to Yinchuan.

Party central? The CCP headquarters in Yinchuan, Ningxia

Huge numbers of mass residential projects have just been completed or are still under construction, both in the spreading suburbs of Yinchuan and in the smaller towns I visited, such as Shizuishan and Lingwu. All of the projects were advertised with fanciful new hoardings promising a world of international sophistication. My favourite announced in large letters "It smells like Britain" (it didn't). The flats in the photograph below on page 16 were selling for between Rmb2,000 and Rmb3,000 per square metre.

Xinhua Department Store is the dominant retailer in Ningxia. It has a market share of roughly 40% of the department store, supermarket and electrical retail sub-sectors. That having been said, most of Ningxia's consumers are currently to be found in Yinchuan, which accounts for 80% of Xinhua's revenues. Same-store sales growth slowed in the first quarter of 2012, but still topped 10% year on year. This reflects a trend we have seen where consumer demand has held up better in central and western China than on the richer east coast. With enlightened management, and finance and technology from shareholder Wumart, the company seems to be holding its own against newcomers. Its next stop is Xining, the capital of neighbouring Qinghai.

Ningxia is not strictly a province. It is actually the "Hui Autonomous Region" (here autonomy to be understood as in "Tibetan autonomy"). I have never before found a listed company owned by a member of a "national minority", so it was a pleasure to visit Zhongyin Cashmere. This business is owned by the three Ma brothers (Ma, literally "horse," is a common Hui surname used to transliterate "Muhammad"). They achieved a listing by injecting the firm into an ST ("Special Treatment" companies that have made losses for 3 successive years) shell company in 2007 (a strategy used by a number of privately owned companies before the opening of the ChiNext market). Since then the company has been winning market share from its better-known state-owned rivals, such as Erdos and Deer King, which have allowed themselves to be diverted into a range of other activities, including coal mining, ferroalloys and property development. Having started as an exporter, the company is developing its own garment brand, Philosofie, for

One-horse town? Despite first impressions, Ningxia shows much of today's China in microcosm.

domestic sales, a trend among China's exporters. Less common, but perhaps a sign of things to come, is its purchase of a Scottish cashmere company, Todd & Duncan. This was not just for the technology, brand or marketing channels; the company continues to manufacture in Kinross. The firm has a high level of debt – mostly used to purchase the raw material – which is unusual for a privately owned company, given the usual reluctance of state-owned banks to lend to them. The clue is in the name: Zhongyin is Chinese shorthand for Bank of China. Back in the 90s, Mr Ma had a joint venture with Bank of China, when the banks were still allowed to do such things. He was allowed to retain the name when he bought the bank out and remains on good terms. To add to the number of unusual things about this company, I could count 12 mosques from the CFO's office window.

In contrast to the positive picture which I have so far painted, I visited a number of state-owned, heavy-industry manufacturers who face a more uncertain future. I first visited a chemical company which makes PVC from coal. It is based in the northern tip of Ningxia, where it borders Inner Mongolia – one of the most polluted places I have ever visited. Industry there is based on the local dirty-coal reserves, so the very ground is black and the air smells of brimstone. In China, PVC is in oversupply, with capacity utilisation running at only about 50%. But the company I visited is running at 100% (they all say that). With credit-tightening, and the slowdown in the property market, the price of PVC plunged in the fourth quarter of 2011 and has so far shown no sign of recovery. Coal costs are rising. The company is barely breaking even. Its answer is to move upmarket to produce PPVC (plasticised PVC), but everything needs to be approved by its parent, the national utility China Guodian, so nothing will happen soon. On the bright side, it was able to get away a highly priced rights issue to its parent last month, raising Rmb1.7 billion to reduce its heavy debt burden. The story was very similar at Ningxia Saima Industrial, the dominant local cement producer with 13 million tons of capacity, which is owned by China Building Materials. There is local overcapacity, the slowdown in demand has caused prices to fall to a low and stay there, and costs are rising. The company, which is still adding capacity, will tough it out and hope for better days.

Another state-owned enterprise's reaction to problems in its main business is to move into someone else's. Orient Tantalum (originally

Factory 905) was moved from Beijing to Ningxia in the 1960s, when Mao feared war with the Soviet Union. It is now one of the world's three largest tantalum-makers (the others being Cabot and Starck), but tantalum has only one main use, in specialist capacitors, and lacks growth potential. In fact, weak demand for electronic exports has meant that volume is down 20% to 30% year on year. So the

"Look on my works, ye mighty ..." The tombs of the Western Xia

company has sunk Rmb1.4 billion into entering the market for titanium (a similar production process to tantalum) and silicon carbide (as the company is bullish on the outlook for the solar industry, where silicon carbide is used for polishing wafers). Unfortunately, Orient's entry has coincided with a slump in the solar industry. Another company smitten by the allure of new energy is Yinxing Energy. After this instrumentation-maker was acquired by the local utility, Ningxia Electricity, in 2006, it charged into the production of wind turbines. With the recent slump in demand, there are now, apparently "only 20 or 30" Chinese turbine-makers left! As turbines have not turned out to be the profit centre they promised to be, the company is now investing in wind farms. Given that these cost Rmb400 million per 50MW installation, the company now has an impressive net gearing of 330%. When asked for the payback period, the spokesman told me, with a straight face, 18 years.

After a prolonged period of double-digit, investment-based economic growth, even a slight slowdown to "only" 8% seems to be undermining the business model of the state-owned enterprises I met. Not that the managements appeared unduly worried – after all, it is not their company, and their jobs are underwritten by influential parents with deep pockets (or at least the ability to put their hands in the pocket of the state-owned banks).

In the fine spring sunshine, Ningxia did not seem too bad a place to live, especially if you like lamb. There are also the remains of ancient cultures to be visited – the Xi Xia tombs and Neolithic engravings in the Helan Pass – which are impressive in an Ozymandias kind of way. The local red wine is also not bad. However, seeing the farmers exhuming acres of old vines (they must be buried to protect against winter temperatures down to -20°C) is a reminder that the weather is not always so clement.

A Letter From Ningxia
12 April 2012
Chris Ruffle

Chapter 4

Pirates at bay

As Shanghai sunk into the cloying embrace of an especially thick smog last week, it wasn't just the buildings that disappeared. Walking home from the metro station, I noticed that something else was missing: the DVD vendors.

The road that takes me back to my flat is usually home to at least a dozen pedlars selling DVDs, Blu Ray discs and CDs from the back of vans or motor-carts. It's all done quite openly, with the wares laid out on stands on the street. The discs are cheap; a DVD costs about 4 kuai (40p), and, if the film's not too recent, they'll generally work fine (or so I'm told ...). The range is startling, with numerous art-house, European and Asian films alongside the Hollywood hits. Purchases of the latest blockbuster are generally ill advised, however: the contents of these discs have usually been filmed in a cinema and include such special features as coughing, whispering and the silhouettes of people getting up to go to the loo. Generally, though, the pirates do a thriving business – some will even take returns when a disc fails to function.

For now, however, the vans and their illicit cargoes are nowhere to be seen. Customs officials launched one of their semi-regular crackdowns last week, with uniformed officers mounting a series of raids. And it wasn't just street pedlars that were affected. Their apparently more respectable cousins, the slick shops that sell DVDs on the same streets, have also been closed down. That shouldn't be a surprise: as far as anyone can tell, the only difference between the merchandise sold from the shops and that sold from the streets is that the shop-bought discs come in fancier, more authentic-looking wrapping (and at a slightly more "respectable" price). Rather ironically, the closed-up shop closest to my apartment still sports a poster for a film called Contraband.

One reason that pirate discs (first VCDs, then DVDs and now Blu Rays) are such a perennial feature of urban China is that there's little direct competition. Only 20 foreign films are approved for distribution each year, hardly sufficient to sate China's growing appetite for new experiences and images. And for a long

Contraband, unfortunately.

time, the big screen was an unappetising alternative to domestic viewing. I remember going to a cinema in Jinan, the capital of Shandong province, in the late 1990s. It was awful. You could hardly see the screen for cigarette smoke, and the film seemed largely incidental to the numerous raucous conversations being conducted in the aisles. I soon walked out (it had cost perhaps a kuai to get in). I have never been tempted back.

But as in so many other areas, the change in Chinese cinemas has been startling. Today, the multiplexes in Chinese shopping malls are a very different breed from the fleapits of a decade ago. They are slick, clean and sophisticated (although a colleague recently found all the jolting and spraying water during a "4D" performance of the re-released Titanic a little much). But of course they're expensive. Tickets for the latest attraction will set you back 80 to 100 kuai a piece. In that context, a 4-kuai DVD is always going to look attractive.

Nor is cost the only consideration. Both cinema releases and legitimate DVDs tend to be heavily censored. A few seconds of naked Kate Winslet failed to make the Chinese cut of the revamped Titanic. And no one will be surprised to learn that anything "politically sensitive" gets snipped. But some other considerations are more surprising: since last year, time travel has been raising censorial hackles. According to Chinese officials, the topic is part of a trend to "casually make up myths, have monstrous and weird plots, use absurd tactics, and even promote feudalism, superstition, fatalism and reincarnation".

Still, sex and nudity tend to be the censors' major concerns – and, it has to be said, a major selling point for the street pirates. Recently, the vendors have been heavily touting the soft-porn Hong Kong flick Sex and Zen 3D: Extreme Ecstasy, while pirate editions of mainstream films often feature cover images that imply they're a great deal naughtier than they actually are. Chinese consumers can watch the hit series Game of Thrones through various perfectly legal online channels for the price of watching a few adverts. But what they won't get is the titillation that the producers have shoehorned in. "I represent the perv side of the audience", a producer reportedly told one of the series' directors; there's no reason for believing that that demographic is smaller in China than anywhere else, and the uncut series is widely available on the streets.

The censors' prudishness is, perhaps inevitably, somewhat behind the times. The preservation of the Winslet modesty provoked a fair degree of scorn from Chinese netizens; the country is, undoubtedly, getting racier. The cover of FHM China's latest edition, for example, features a topless mermaid, albeit with her back turned to the camera. And at last month's recent Beijing Auto Fair, it wasn't just the tyres that were pneumatic: thanks to the presence of scantily clad models, including the buxom internet celebrity Gan Lulu, the event drew official condemnation for what some microbloggers described as "a breast show with some cars thrown in". Meanwhile an advert for the travel agent Elong appears to suggest that an attractive couple have been sharing something more than a smouldering glance in an elevator. As the ad is shown on screens in office elevators, I've yet to figure out quite what response it's meant to provoke; perhaps fortunately, the workers in Citigroup Tower appear unmoved.

In fact, official censors are probably little concerned with the morals of office workers or other sophisticated adults. The real thrust of most non-political censorship in the media is towards children, particularly teenagers. Why? Because they should be hard at work studying, not idling away their time with leisure pursuits. That is the most likely explanation for the authorities' antagonism towards time travel: the fantasy series Gong, in which a contemporary girl travels back to the Qing court, was a massive hit last year; parents of ardent fans who should have been doing their homework were not impressed. Official disapproval is one way of telling China's ambitious and often rather conservative parents that "we hear you".

And with the country's 18-year-olds knuckling down last week to the gaokao, the gruelling three-day exam marathon that decides their educational future, the crackdown on illicit DVDs might just have been a symbolic gesture to reassure parents that in this of all weeks, no distractions would be tolerated.

A Letter China
14 June 2012
Justin Crozier

Chapter 5

Weighty matters

The countdown to the Olympics is well underway here in China. The London Games are already a feature in TV ads, as manufacturers of sportswear and isotonic drinks milk the event for all it's worth. China is excited. And it has good reason to be. After collecting 51 gold medals in Beijing, the sporting superpower is well placed for another stellar run this summer. For this, Chinese sports fans will be grateful. Despite the palpable desires of 1.3 billion, the nation's football team hasn't delivered: November's defeat by Iraq was just the latest in a string of disappointments.

But the Chinese Olympic squad is a very different prospect. Four years ago, at its own sporting showpiece, China's athletes topped the table, with 100 medals overall. Nowhere was this success more evident than in gymnastics (10 golds) and weightlifting, where Chinese lifters snatched (and cleaned and jerked) eight golds in 15 weight categories.

In global terms, China's success at weightlifting is something of an anomaly. Most countries that excel at weightlifting have a substantial grass-roots culture from which to recruit their champions. Iran's ancient zoorkaneh tradition has survived the sweeping prohibitions of the ayatollahs, while Bulgaria, Turkey and Russia all have long traditions of gym-going, dating back centuries and amply attested to in literature. (In

Tolstoy's Anna Karenina, for example, the progressive landowner Levin keeps dumbbells in his study, can lift "thirteen stone with one hand" and is nonplussed by the unmanliness of the civil servant Grinevitch, with his slender hand and long, curling fingernails. More of that later …) In these countries, the thousands of recreational athletes hefting iron at local gyms form a substantial talent pool from which high-level competitors emerge.

But not in China. It's demonstrably the best country in the world at weightlifting, with astonishing athletes such as world champions Tian Yuan (women's 48kg) and Liu Xiaolong (men's 77kg) poised to grace the platform at the London Olympics. But try finding a local weightlifting competition, even in a vast metropolis like Shanghai or Beijing. There simply aren't any. And even decent weightlifting gymnasia are few and far between. China makes some of the best barbells, plates and platforms in the world, but they're rarely to be glimpsed in gyms here.

World-champion weightlifter Liu Xiaolong

What explains this? Obviously, China's top-level athletes are a key source of national pride, and the government puts an enormous emphasis on international success. So most of the country's sporting programmes are top-down, rather than bottom-up. And, with trophies the key consideration, the likelihood of success is all-important. I recently heard that in the nascent international sport of touch rugby, the Chinese sporting authorities have decided to focus on women's, rather than men's, teams, because their chances of competitive glory are reckoned to be higher.

This top-down focus means that prospects are scouted out and then put onto intensive development programmes. This can work well for individual sports, but less well for team sports, where the creativity and off-the-cuff instincts forged by endless days of playing in parks and backyards are all important. China, of course, has relatively few backyards, and while its parks are fine places for flying kites, ball sports tend to be discouraged: hence, perhaps, the relative failure of its football team.

But park attendants and their wish to preserve the grass are not the only discouragement that budding Chinese sportspeople face. A far greater threat to incipient sporting prowess than lack of space comes from parents. Sports, to many of China's child-rearing millions, are simply a waste of time – time that could far more productively be spent on study. For Chinese schoolchildren, the spectre of the gaokao – the university entrance exam – is inescapable.

For the parents, it's a simple equation. Study equals success. Success equals wealth. And wealth equals both happiness for the child and support for the parents in their old age. In this stark life-cycle, sports don't get a look-in. So there's certainly an element of discouragement of anything that might seem like an excessive interest in physical pastimes.

Intertwined with this, there's also what one might call a rather longstanding anti-athletic strand in Chinese culture. A spot of anthropological theorising might trace this to the fact that China has, for hundreds of years if not for millennia, been a scholar-aristocratic country rather than a warrior-aristocratic one. While the European gentry were hunting (practising for war), shooting (practising for war) or fencing (practising for war), their Chinese counterparts were studying – preparing for the civil-service entry exams – or writing poetry. Like today's gaokao, the civil-service exams, with their eight-legged essays, cast a long shadow over the nation's educated classes. And unlike today's gaokao, that civil-service examination could haunt and taunt an ambitious man for life. The Qing-era ghost-story writer Pu Songling spent decades in vain attempts to improve his status through the examination system; his entire literary output was a side-product of this.

The most vivid portrait of the human misery that the system could cause comes from a more modern writer, Lu Xun. His famous story Kong Yiji vividly describes a ruined scholar, frustrated in his ambitions and reduced to theft and beggary – but yet too proud to earn an honest living as a labourer. Lu Xun's scornful narrator describes the eponymous Kong as having "overextended fingernails" – much like Tolstoy's Grinevitch.

Kong Yiji's long fingernails, like his robe (reduced to tatters by the time of the story), show that he is above working with his hands. Whatever else he has become, he is not a menial labourer or peasant. This display of status became thoroughly institutionalised during the Qing dynasty, as China's Manchu rulers, originally tough nomadic warriors from the north, became Sinicised scholar-aristocrats, silk-robed, long-nailed and – very much – above working. Indeed, the Qing bannermen, originally warrior-aristocrats, enjoyed a status that explicitly elevated them above working with their hands, even once they had lost their warrior function. And so these Manchus became more Chinese than the Chinese themselves.

These hands ain't made for working ...

The effete and – to Western eyes at least – effeminate Qing bannerman was the root of a great deal of Orientalist stereotyping in the West. Of course, the otiose Qing aristocrats were only part of the story. Modernising and revolutionary Chinese despised what they saw as their sickly, decadent rulers. As well as Lu Xun's sympathy, you can feel his contempt for the unfortunate Kong. Lu Xun had taken up jiu-jitsu in Japan – a country which, with its tough, energetic ways, he saw as providing a model for China.

Sun Yat-sen agreed. The revolutionary, whom all Chinese (on both sides of the Formosa straits) acknowledge as a national hero, urged his countrymen to achieve "competent governance of the natural functions" – controlling belching and farting, refraining from spitting in public and ending the practice of growing fingernails to "unsightly lengths".

But despite the universal acclaim in which Sun is held (just about every Chinese city has a Zhongshan park; he is known as Sun Zhongshan on the mainland), this advice hasn't received universal take-up. In particular, taxi drivers very often sport long nails on their thumbs and little fingers; as some of the first small businessmen to be allowed to operate under Deng Xiaoping's reforms, these were the original Chinese wide boys.

The message is "no manual labourer here" – and indeed, taxi drivers were highly sought after as husbands in the 1980s. So Chinese taxi drivers are, in this small way at least, upholding the traditions of China's scholar-aristocracy. And men who grow their fingernails to remarkable lengths are unlikely to do much in the way of sport.

But this traditional – and to Western eyes unmanly – model of manliness is far from universal. Today's scholars tend to be more Lu Xun than Kong Yiji. Ironically, the hands that advertise disdain for manual work tend to belong to working-class boys made good rather than genuine "intellectuals" (which, for today's Chinese, generally translates as "graduates").

There are, however, other ways in which the "anti-athletic" culture still hangs in the foggy air of urban China. While height is considered a highly desirable quality in a potential husband or wife, brains are very much preferred to brawn. Under pressure from their parents and from society at large, China's eligible bachelorettes are a notoriously picky bunch. And one common requirement is that potential suitors should not be "too strong". Perhaps influenced by the country's innumerable androgynous pop stars as well as by lingering connotations of physical labouring and poor education, the xiaojie about town generally prefers svelteness to

Lu Zhishen uproots a tree in The Water Margin

muscles (or so several rugby-playing Chinese friends of mine regularly report). And potential parents-in-law might baulk at a physique that suggested more devotion to sports than study: unless the suitor in question is a professional sportsman, it could suggest diminished economic prospects. A weedy baimian xuesheng ("white-faced scholar"), on the other hand, could well be a desirable match. And at least one study has suggested that the paunch as signifier of wealth has a persistent, albeit diminishing, appeal.

But while one model of Chinese masculinity is of the successful, portly official (or, these days, businessman) with his soft and long-nailed hands, there's a parallel model of similar longevity. Look at any Chinese kung-fu movie and you'll see it: the humble, hard-working and honest toiler who defies corrupt officialdom. Over the centuries, representatives of this paradigm have included martial artists, outlaws, rebels and revolutionaries. In contrast to the plump, silk-clad officials, the archetypal rebel/outlaw/revolutionary is not afraid to get his hands dirty. Rather, he is vigorous, hardy and, of course, athletic.

Nowhere is this contrast better embodied than Shui Hu, in one of China's four great classic novels, known in English as The Outlaws of the Marsh or The Water Margin. In the novel, which has some parallels to Britain's legends of Robin Hood, the doughty outlaws outwit corrupt officials before eventually winning a pardon from the Emperor himself. Along the way, they brawl, hunt tigers, and uproot trees.

It's easy to see a parallel to the vigorous outlaws of The Water Margin in the Boxer Rebellion of 1898 to 1901. The Boxers – known to themselves as the Society of the Righteous and Harmonious Fists – were so-called by foreigners because of their devotion to martial arts and other forms of physical training. Their bloody rebellion against the Qing government and foreign powers, together with its equally bloody suppression, is one of the most disputed areas of Chinese history. Revolutionaries such as Sun Yat-sen had mixed views of the Boxers, balancing disapproval of their mysticism and xenophobia to approval of their courage and spirit.

But it's not hard to see the likes of Sun Yat-sen, Lu Xun and of course the young Mao Zedong (on whom some maintain The Water Margin had a

Boxer rebels: these chaps didn't worry about breaking a nail ....

significant influence) as owing something to the tradition of vigorous, physically disciplined rebels. Certainly, they shared a disgust with the corrupt and comfortable ways of China's established rulers. And the monumental sculptures of Red China, with their muscular workers and righteous fists, have more in common with the burly outlaws of the marsh (and of course Soviet Russia) than the fluttering robes of the mandarins.

In today's China, though, the mandarin model of masculinity is probably in the ascendant once more; anywhere where well-heeled Chinese flock, you'll see more Grinevitches than Levins. But change is the only constant here. Gyms, and gym memberships, are becoming more and more common, and there's little evidence of "anti-athletic" culture among the country's legions of high-flying graduates. Further successes in the London Olympics can only encourage athletic pursuits – and as more Chinese achieve a comfortable standard of living, the mad rush for wealth will likely give way to a desire for a more balanced life. This tends to happen in any case: with their taijiquan, morning callisthenics and dancing, China's senior citizens must be among the most active in the world. And perhaps one day soon, it might even be possible to find a gym with some decent weightlifting equipment ...

A Letter China
21 June 2012
Justin Crozier

Chapter 6

Urban wildlife

At first glance, the dominant tone of any Chinese cityscape is grey. Grey buildings under grey skies, with only the floods of neon after dark to enliven the outlook. But if you look a little closer, there's generally plenty of green there too. Not only are there parks (not as many as there should be, admittedly), but housing complexes tend to be fairly leafy, with an abundance of trees and bushes to offer shade in summer and at least the semblance of a natural environment.

And, to some extent, this kind of "green" urban planning works. Where I live, in the centre of Shanghai's Pudong area, there are tower-blocks in virtually every direction as far as the eye can see (which, when the pollution is bad, isn't particularly far). But at night, the compound is alive with the sound of frogs. Bats flicker around the buildings and chase moths around the streetlamps (in China, bats are a good omen, as the Chinese word for bat is a homophone for "luck"). And by day, the ponds in which my children paddle are squirming with tadpoles.

The arrival of morning is reinforced by birdsong – and at considerable volume. Urban China is home to a surprisingly wide range of bird species, including various strikingly coloured finches. Most striking of all are the azure-winged magpies that frequent the leafy compounds and campuses of Chinese metropolises.

Azure-winged magpies in Shanghai

Of course, there are abundant insects too – not just the mosquitos that plague the human population in the summer, but crickets, cicadas and pond-skaters, as well as large numbers of butterflies. As we walked to his nursery the other day, my son drew my attention to a "watermelon ant". It turned out to be what in Scotland we would call a "slater": the small arthropod known more widely as a woodlouse. In China, the creature is known as a xigua chong ("watermelon insect") because it looks a little like a black watermelon seed.

The woodlouse's rather poetic name here is typical. There's a tremendous lyricism to many Chinese animal names. A gecko is a bihu or "wall tiger". An owl is a maotouying, or "cat-headed hawk". And the stink bug, which poses an occasional olfactory threat around Chinese homes, is known as chou dajie – "stinky big sister".

More prosaically, there are also large populations of feral animals in Chinese cities. Most housing compounds – and many parks – are home to feral cats. They do at least help to keep rats and mice under control. Many ponds are home to turtles; most or all of these are released pets, and not all are native species. Dogs are generally kept on a tighter leash, with the authorities regularly rounding up unlicensed pets. Predictably, this has caused some consternation among China's foreign residents, but the aim is to prevent outbreaks of rabies.

Of course, the diversity of the urban menagerie is put to shame by a visit to any respectably sized restaurant, where tankfuls of fish, snakes, frogs, turtles and eels wriggle and clamber over each other. Legions of shrimps spar among themselves on the floors of aquaria. And in some establishments there are larger crustaceans too: enormous crabs and lobsters, or long xia: "dragon shrimps."

Arresting though the Chinese names for various animals are, I often notice that the Chinese tend to be much less specific about types of animal than English speakers are. Certainly, there's more use of generic names here: more or less any rodent can be called a "mouse", while just about anything that lives in the water is a "fish" (a giant salamander, for example, is an "infant

Here's looking at you, babe: the "infant fish"

fish", because it makes a crying noise like a child). Experience (chiefly acquired through the constant questioning of a bilingual three-year-old) has taught me that even educated people here won't generally be able to name, say, a wolverine (native to China) or a tapir (native to Malaysia rather than China, but featured in Chinese mythology). None of my colleagues, for example, knew offhand the Chinese name for the azure-winged magpies; they were simply "birds".

All that changes, though, once animals end up on a plate. Thanks to Aristotle, Europeans may have a wide range of animal names; the Eskimos, sadly, do not actually have 50 words for snow. But the Chinese certainly have an enormous vocabulary when it comes to eating, with a wealth of specific terms for ingredients and a wonderful range of allusive names for completed dishes. Indeed, I think that the specificity of terms for food can sometimes render English translations of modern Chinese novels rather clunky, with long hyphenated strings "unpacking" the original terms.

Recently, a colleague jocularly suggested that the obvious solution to the problem of stray cats and unlicensed dogs in Shanghai would be shipping them all off to Guangdong (Canton). According to other Chinese at least, the Cantonese, eat "anything with four legs except the table and anything that flies except an aeroplane". Wouldn't consignments of unwanted pets therefore be met with open woks? I can claim no knowledge of the Cantonese language, but I know that there are divergences from Mandarin in vocabulary as well as the obvious – and substantial – differences in pronunciation). I sometimes wonder whether the famously broad appetites of Guangdong's residents equip them with a wider range of zoological terms than their northern neighbours.

In any case, the hum of cicadas and the solemn chanting of frogs provide the welcome, if improbable, illusion of country living – even in the heart of the densest megacity. Background music isn't the only way in which they interact with their human neighbours, though: you don't have to go to Guangdong to find cicadas (cooked in honey) or frogs on your dinner plate.

A Letter China
26 June 2012
Justin Crozier

Chapter 7

Issues of transparency

The big story in Shanghai this week was the controversial message posted on Shanghai Metro's weibo microblog. It contained a photo of a young woman standing on the platform, wearing a see-through dress which revealed black underwear. According to the Metro administrators, she was setting a bad example. The accompanying text read: "Girls – please maintain your dignity to avoid perverts".

Skimpy clothing is certainly nothing new in Shanghai. Indeed, people from other parts of China say that "There's nothing that the Cantonese won't eat or the Shanghainese won't wear." In the summer at least, skirts are short and shorts are shorter. Of course, as many young women interviewed by journalists in the wake of the Metro warning pointed out, there's good reason for this: it's hot.

And, as the summer humidity builds, nowhere is it hotter than on Line 6 of the Metro in the rush hour – despite the underground air conditioning. Line 6 stretches north into the suburbs of Pudong, Shanghai's recently developed east bank; by the time the train reaches more central residential areas, it's jam-packed with commuters.

That dress

Indeed, one of Shanghai's most disheartening experiences is reaching the platform to find other commuters there in any sort of number. That generally means that there's been a delay – usually nothing that would register as such on the London Underground, perhaps just a minute or two. But it means that the train, when it arrives, will be even more crowded than usual. And so, most likely, will the next one.

When the doors open, there's no obvious space: people fill the carriage right to the groove of the doors. And until the train reaches the Century Avenue stop, virtually no one gets off. To get on, you simply have to push yourself into the crowd.

And when you get to the next station, the doors slide open again, and there are people on the platform eyeing the sweating mass of bodies and bracing themselves to push into its heart – which they do. And so on, until the train reaches Century Avenue, where it disgorge at least half of its contents. Me included: I get to switch to Line 2, which is a good deal less crammed (you generally are afforded a little space in which to stand).

Many expats in Shanghai are vocal about the appalling rudeness of Metro commuters. I don't see it; given the circumstances, people seem to be extraordinarily patient and polite. True, there is a great deal of pushing and shoving. But otherwise, there's simply no way to get on or off the more crowded trains. This morning was a case in point: a lady of a certain girth was one of very few getting off the Line 6 train before Century Avenue. She issued an impassioned apology – "Bu hao yisi!" – before dropping her shoulder and ramming her way onto the platform. If she hadn't, the train would have been off before she was.

Still, it's always good to be braced for the impact of one's fellow-passengers. Last week, I was swept bodily from the train before my stop. This wasn't a result of barging by any individual, but simply the collective drive of the twenty or so behind me who needed to disembark. To be upset by it would be to take arms against a sea of (individually blameless) travellers. Happily, no one does.

Underground behaviour isn't entirely exemplary, though. The weibo message from Shanghai Metro appears to have been prompted by the recent arrest of a flasher (not on Line 6: no one would have had room to notice). And there have been other recent reports of sexual harassment on the trains. But given the sheer volume of passengers, such unwelcome incidents seem almost remarkably infrequent. Certainly, China doesn't have anything like Japan's notorious chikan problem. Some upstanding Chinese subway-users have, however, borrowed one habit from the Japanese: conspicuous reading, with both hands on a mobile device (to prove that those hands are not wandering elsewhere).

Of course, as numerous bloggers have pointed out, what people wear has little to do with whether or not they are subjected to harassment. And China is not a country in which people worry overmuch about bared flesh. In southern Europe, British and UK tourists often stand out (and are sometimes mocked) because they wear shorts and t-shirts while the natives manage to stay cool in long trousers and shirts. But the Chinese have no qualms about stripping down to singlets and shorts in the heat (bare-chested men are a frequent sight in the summer). Indeed, the Han Chinese preference for skimpy summer-wear may exacerbate tensions in provinces with large Muslim populations.

In part, the Chinese preference for revealing clothes is a celebration of the freedom to wear what you like. Older people remember Mao's China, when dress was uniform and uniformly modest (even down to rules on how hair was worn: cropped or braided only) – and many are relieved that their children don't suffer from the same constraints.

Such is the wide acceptance of light clothing that the presence of the US "breastaurant" chain Hooters has caused little or no fuss in China. Contrast that with the media hullaballoo and protests that accompanied the recent opening of two branches in the UK: both have now closed. But the Shanghai branch, just around the corner from our office, is uncontroversial. The low-cut tops and orange hot-pants of the waitresses hardly stand out – after all, they're little different from what many young women are wearing on the subway.

What was perhaps most interesting about the Shanghai Metro story was how familiar it sounded to Western ears. Like so many British and US public figures before them, the Metro administrators made a clumsy statement that appeared to be blaming victims for inciting crimes. And, just as in the West, citizens and, especially, netizens reacted scornfully. There was even a protest on the subway, with a couple of women holding up slogans that translated as "We can dress sexily; you can't molest us" – echoing last year's SlutWalk marches in the US and UK. The state newspapers were even-handed in their coverage, and while Shanghai Metro didn't apologise, a spokesman insisted that they weren't telling anyone what to wear, just trying to keep the public safe. Don't expect to see changes in Shanghainese hemlines any time soon!

A Letter From China
29 June 2012
Justin Crozier

Chapter 8

Going native

In English, "throbbing" and "heaving" might be positive words when applied to nightclubs (if you like that sort of thing). In Chinese, an equivalent term, renao (literally "hot and noisy"), can be used approvingly of some quite different establishments – supermarkets, for example.

In a crowded country, people often prefer the rumbustious and even the raucous to the refined. This is perhaps a result of China's agricultural heritage: after a hard day in the fields, a noisy conviviality allows people to blow off steam. Foreign companies that do well in China have generally taken note of local tastes. A good example is the French hypermarket chain Carrefour. There are numerous branches in most major Chinese cities, and they have managed to create the requisite renao atmosphere. This has been done quite deliberately, through the narrowing of aisles, the piling high of goods and the cranking up of music. Carrefour's Chinese stores are loud and bustling – and popular. By contrast, the UK pharmacy chain Boots was a notable failure in China, where people were put off by its spacious, clinical aisles.

But conjuring a sufficiently renao atmosphere is just one of the ways in which Carrefour has successfully "localized". Cynics might point to the fines it recently received for pricing fraud in Wuhan as the best proof of this, or the fact that it has just opened a Communist Party office in one of its Beijing outlets, but the chain has taken on other Chinese characteristics too.

Most obviously, it has adopted the entire menagerie of the Chinese "wet market". Walk into any of Carrefour's Chinese branches and you'll find a central location devoted to tank upon tank of live shrimps, fish, crabs, turtles and bullfrogs (viewings of which make for a good reward for children dragged unwillingly to the supermarket ...).

Food for thought ...

Some other changes are more cosmetic: the distinctly Chinese stalls in the crowded aisles, for example. But they still show that Carrefour is at pains to match the Chinese consumer's expectations.

And that's the key thing. "Chinese characteristics" are proving remarkably robust. In a globalised age, it's all too easy to assume that tastes are converging around the globe into a kind of bland, vaguely

Anglo-European, consensus. There is certainly an element of this. In the past decade or so, for example, China has taken to coffee and wine with gusto: no longer do the Chinese prefer their red wine mixed with Sprite, and cafés are now ubiquitous in Chinese cities. But in many other matters, Chinese preferences are firmly entrenched. Foreign companies do well to pay attention.

Food is an obvious example. One of the greatest success stories in the decades since Deng Xiaoping initiated his reforms is KFC. The Colonel is big in China; after the chain opened its Tiananmen Square branch in 1987, it quickly acquired a sort of luxury cachet that was somewhat at odds with its status in the West: in 1990s China, for example, KFC was seen as a good place for a first date.

Today, it's the largest Western restaurant chain operating in the country (bigger than MacDonald's, crucially), with more than 4,000 branches. On the face of it, it's an unlikely success: one wouldn't expect a downmarket fast-food chain to succeed in a nation globally renowned for its cuisine – and which has a remarkable street-food culture to complement its haute cuisine. But a large part of KFC's success lies in the way in which it has adapted to local tastes.

Would y'all like some congee with your chicken?

Alongside the familiar fried chicken and burgers, Chinese KFC outlets offer rice dishes, fried breadsticks and a variety of congees. Colonel Sanders might not be turning in his ample grave, but he'd certainly be hard-pushed to recognise most of this stuff. For Chinese customers, of course, it's the best of both worlds: a taste of Kentucky alongside plenty of familiar comforts. The branch near me always seems to be doing a roaring trade at breakfast time.

Where Carrefour and KFC have succeeded is in giving Chinese consumers what they want. But another company has localised in China through taking a slightly different approach: giving its Chinese customers what they need. The company is Ikea, and the need that it's meeting is space. For many millions in urban China, living space is a prized commodity. Ask anyone here about where they live and you'll get it in square metres. I don't know anyone in the UK who knows the area of the rooms of their home offhand; I don't know anyone in China who doesn't.

Ikea has honed in on this expertly. Its stores are decorated with a series of "It's Our Home" features that show how Swedish "solutions" can maximise space in Chinese homes. The examples range from a young couple in their first bedsit to a three-generation family sharing a single flat. Ikea's signature bunk beds, folding tables and hidden storage all have obvious applications here. And, after an initial period when most visitors came to sightsee, socialise or even sleep in the stores, the company is reaping the rewards of meeting one of urban China's most pressing needs, with sales up strongly in 2011 and 2012.

Indeed, the company has been paid the ultimate compliment (or at least the sincerest form of flattery), with an "11 Furniture" store in Kunming that aped the Swedish chain even down to its blue and yellow livery. Nor is the Kunming store the only counterfeit Ikea around. When my son's bed fell apart the other day, I found that it had been held together with knock-offs of the Swedish firm's signature clamps. Unfortunately, they didn't work as well.

And Ikea's in-store cafés are a big hit in China too. Free refills are something of a novelty in China, and the free coffee that came with an Ikea loyalty card proved such an attraction that one Shanghai branch had to take measures to control a large and rowdy group of senior citizens who congregated in its restaurant each week.

Eating in the café of the Pudong branch the other week, I was unsurprised that the menu included a couple of noodle and rice dishes alongside the customary meatballs. I was, however, somewhat surprised to see that French fries were off the menu; the meatballs were served with mashed potatoes only. But then it occurred to me that I had no idea what Ikea serves in Sweden, but only what it serves in Scotland. Could it be, I wondered, that the choice of chips in the company's Edinburgh store is simply another example of successful localisation? Ikea may very well have reasoned that no one ever lost money selling fried food to the Scots ...

A Letter From China
10 July 2012
Justin Crozier

Chapter 9

Outside on the inside

After living in Shanghai for a decade and a half, Mrs Li is well acquainted with the sprawling megacity. She has worked in dozens of jobs in the city and raised her children there. Yet she is still not well acquainted with her neighbours – because they won't speak to her or her husband. The reason? She and her family are waidi ren (or nga di nyin in Shanghainese), literally "outside people". And in the working-class neighbourhood of Shanghai in which she lives, this puts her beyond the pale.

Many of the city's better-heeled natives would be surprised at this. Shanghai is China's most cosmopolitan city and is famously proud of this status. Foreigners come to the city in their droves to work in education, industry and finance; students from across China enrol in its universities and colleges; and its factories, shops and local-government services depend on migrant workers like Mrs Li. So why the resentment?

One reason is the same the world over. Those in low-paid jobs feel under threat from migrants (whether from the same country or not) who are willing to work harder and accept lower pay. For a Shanghainese, a low-paid job is a sign of failure: evidence that you have been left behind as the city surges forward. For migrants, on the other hand, low-paid work is a rung on a ladder – albeit a tall one with many, many rungs. Sometimes, real upward progress might only be made by the next generation, if at all. Mrs Li works in catering, cleaning and childcare, juggling several jobs at the same time; her husband works in a factory. But their two children are doing somewhat better (her son is a dim sum chef at an upmarket hotel) – and the next generation can expect to do better still.

A further rift comes from the fact that a significant number of poorer Shanghainese do no work at all. The benefits system in the big cities provides enough of a safety net for people in certain circumstances to get by. Often, these are people who have taken very early retirement from state-owned concerns and who have missed out on the economic opportunities of recent decades. For Shanghai-ren who are resigned to an existence on benefits, the fact that they have to live cheek by jowl with hardworking waidi ren entails an additional loss of face – and source of resentment.

An irony here is that many – indeed most – of today's Shanghainese are themselves recent descendants of waidi ren. All of Shanghai's net population growth over the past couple of decades has come from migrants; there are three times as many as there were in the early 1990s. And most "authentic" Shanghainese have only a generation or two to distinguish their pedigrees. The city's population was only 5 million in 1949; today it is not far off five times that.

One of the most striking things about the Shanghainese is their dialect, which, to all intents and purposes is a distinct language. But most speakers of Shanghainese have learned it from parents or grandparents for whom it was not the mother tongue. Oddly enough, only in certain rural suburbs is truly authentic Shanghaihua widely spoken. Nevertheless, fluency in the dialect allows Shanghai natives a sense of belonging that excludes those who have moved to the city to work.

Despite their un-neighbourly Shanghai neighbours, Mrs Li and her husband have come to dread their annual visits home to the rural county in Anhui province where they both grew up. While they suffer in the big city from their status as outsiders, in the countryside they are seen as having "made it" by virtue of their residence and employment in Shanghai. And that means that they are obliged to give gifts of money – and not only to members of their immediate family. Cousins, neighbours and even the boyfriends and girlfriends of fairly distant relatives are all keen to share in the supposed wealth of the high rollers from the big city.

But by the standards of rural Anhui, Mrs Li is well off. In today's China the variability of costs is huge. This is stark enough within the big cities (depending where you buy it, a beer in Shanghai can cost you 2 yuan or 80 yuan; I put that into context by imagining what it would be like if the price of a pint ranged from £2 to £80 in the UK!). But the contrast between city and countryside is simply extraordinary. What her Anhui relatives fail to understand is that her "high" earnings don't go very far in the Big Smoke.

That sort of misunderstanding is just part of a further problem for China's millions of migrant workers. People like Mrs Li's children – born in the city but not official residents – face a sort of double dislocation. They are not fully part of Shanghai, but nor are they at home in their rural "hometowns", which lack the urban facilities and comforts with which they have grown up: internet cafes, cinemas and karaoke bars, for example.

Compounding the difficulties that such second-generation migrants face is the hukou system. China's internal passport is often said to be on its last legs, but for migrants from rural areas, it remains a considerable problem. Although there is now more flexibility than there once was (and a greater degree of regional variation), migrant workers often have little access to healthcare or education for their children – hence the vast numbers of children who remain with grandparents in their hometowns while their parents seek work in the cities.

Indeed, attempts to improve this situation often meet with fierce resistance from local residents. Shanghai now claims to provide free education for all migrant workers' children – but online forums show that some permanent residents feel aggrieved that waidi ren are getting easy access to local education when locals have had to scrimp and save to buy houses close to good schools. Protective urban parents (and the one-child policy has fostered some extremes of mollycoddling) also fret that their tender offspring will be exposed to the roughhousing ways of "hard disk" kids.

Ying pan, or "hard disk" is Shanghai internet slang for "migrant". As many bulletin boards banned waidi ren as a derogatory term, along with its abbreviation WDR, users circumvented this by first using WD, which was difficult to censor because it was also used for the company West Digital. And because West Digital makes hard disks, ying pan became the snide urbanite's slur of choice.

Fortunately, the internet offers migrants more than a channel for abuse. Increasingly, the web is allowing transient workers the opportunity to pick and choose their employers, with sites such as daguu.com providing reviews of working conditions, including wages, dormitories and canteens. Developments of this kind will certainly put upward pressure on manufacturing wages, as they help migrants to explore options in the service industry rather than just factory or construction work. To compete, manufacturers and building firms will need to improve conditions – which can only be a good thing.

After all, it's China's armies of migrants who have provided the muscle and sweat to build the gleaming skyscrapers of the east-coast metropolises, and who are currently toiling on infrastructure projects and new cities in the inland. So far, they have largely been denied a share in the fruits of their labour. With urban China dependent on migrants to – quite literally – do its dirty work, the authorities are aware that discontent arising from the privileged status of urban natives will need to be diffused. Of all the tensions in contemporary Chinese society, that between urban residents and migrant workers is perhaps the most acute.

For Mrs Li, the reforms necessary for more than a basic level of comfort will probably come too late. But for her children and grandchildren, the prospects are likely to be considerably brighter. As Shanghainese speakers brought up in the city, they can, at the very least, hope for more cordial relations with their neighbours.

A Letter From China
25 July 2012
Justin Crozier

Chapter 10

Speaking your language

Recent tests by the Organisation for Economic Cooperation and Development ranked Chinese schoolchildren top of the world in maths and science. This surprised precisely no one: ample column inches have been devoted to the extraordinary success of Chinese pupils in numerical disciplines. Theories explaining this prowess have ranged from the superior logic of Chinese numerals to the mathematical effort required in the cultivation of rice (though no one appears to have told that to the wheat-growing northern Chinese).

Less heralded, however, is the success that Chinese schools and universities have had in teaching English. Indeed, Chinese speakers of English have to contend with a reputation for butchering the language: "Chinglish" has become an international comic phenomenon, with mistranslated signs a staple of light relief in the Western media. That's not to say that there aren't plenty of outlandishly odd snippets of English floating about in China. My favourite is the sign on an upmarket hairdresser's salon near Shanghai's Yuyuan Gardens that offers, among various hair treatments, "blow satisfaction" (although this establishment looks perfectly respectable, many hairdressers in China have a reputation for providing services that diverge considerably from the short back and sides ...).

> # 适量取用　您节约的不仅是一张纸
> ## Use Tissue Sparingly To Spare A Tree

Could you do better in Mandarin?

Of course, it's only the bad translations that catch the eye; plenty of perfectly serviceable ones pass unnoticed. And there is a colossal amount of English-language signage in China. Indeed, sometimes, the translations are actually rather good. In the toilets of Citigroup Towers, for instance, the sign above the paper hand-towels has a certain poetic elegance:

And while it's easy to mock inept English signage, it's just as easy to forget that the Chinese translations increasingly employed at British tourist attractions are often equally bad (my wife reports that some of the Mandarin text at Edinburgh Castle is downright inept).

We should remember, too, how big a gulf there is between the Chinese and English languages – and that most of China's English signs have been written by Chinese translators, rather than by native speakers of English. Inevitably, this leads to some stylistic oddities, as well as to some cringeworthy howlers. After all, most native English speakers confine their language learning to other Indo-European tongues, rather than braving anything so far-flung as the Sino-Tibetan group to which Chinese belongs.

So it's all the more impressive that the Chinese education system produces thousands upon thousands of graduates who are remarkably accomplished English speakers. This is achieved methodically. In the big cities, many Chinese children start to learn English at kindergarten and have exposure to native-speaker teachers from as young as age three. Intensive study follows at school. Then, if they go on to college or university, they will have regular English classes for another three or four years. Chinese teaching is often criticised for being overly dependent on rote learning and call-and-response methods, but, if judged by the myriad graduates who attend top-rated Western universities, it works.

And those high-profile students are just the cream of the crop. Take a train journey in China, and you'll inevitably find people eager and able to speak to you in English. Plenty of street pedlars have a fair bit of the language at their disposal, as do most service-sector workers under 40. The intensity of English teaching and the fact that it lasts right the way through tertiary education have given China a vast pool of competent English speakers. Try to imagine a US or UK in which every college graduate was fluent in Chinese (it takes some doing!).

It's worth noting, too, that at many Chinese universities, the best English speakers aren't necessarily the English majors. A saying that has been doing the rounds in Chinese universities for decades runs like this: "Science students look down on language students; language students look down on history students; history students look down on politics students; politics students look down on their teachers." Often, the best science and engineering students are accomplished all-rounders who see fluency in English as a necessary accessory for a career in research or industry.

The total number of English speakers in China is a matter of some dispute. Reportedly, some 300 million are studying the language. The number of genuine "speakers" was estimated at a mere 10 million in

2006 – although in the intervening six years, one would expect a large number of the learners to have achieved some mastery of the language.

One effect of this has been to create an educated elite that is practically bilingual. Within the glittering towers of Lujiazui, for example, are vast numbers of Chinese professionals who are entirely comfortable in using English in their business dealings. Many of them have cemented their language skills by studying in the US or the UK. Conversations in elevators and offices are often peppered with English words and phrases; in many cases, people prefer to use English technical terms without bothering to translate them into Chinese. They can do so in the knowledge that their interlocutors will understand them perfectly well. It might even be argued that English occupies a similar position to that which French did among the intelligentsia and aristocracy of Russia and Great Britain in the 18th and 19th century.

Certainly, Chinese language learning has come a long way in the past few decades. In the 1980s, the best students would memorize every entry on each page of a dictionary, tearing out the pages that they had internalised as they went. This rather zealous approach signalled a time when English was seen as an absolute must – and as a formidable challenge. There were worries at the time that computers would not be able to handle Chinese characters, and that complete technical mastery of English was a must for the modern world.

Around 20 years ago, "English corners" were all the rage in Chinese cities. As people realised that memorising dictionaries and rote learning didn't do much for conversational skills, meeting places for freeflowing English conversation sprang up in public parks and playgrounds. These were usually hectic, crowded gatherings, with countless simultaneous conversations conducted across each other. Any foreigners who attended were inevitably mobbed with questions and introductions (for native speakers, claiming to be from a non-English-speaking nation was often necessary). The "Crazy English" phenomenon that encourages learning through shouting has its roots in the boisterous atmosphere of 1990s language-learning.

Happily, things are a little more relaxed today. While Crazy English is still going strong, the surviving "English corners" generally have a different purpose now, serving as an arena for matchmaking (a Chinese obsession to be discussed in a future letter!). In large part, this is simply because many Chinese people have realised that mastering English is not that difficult. "People see it now as just another skill – like learning to drive," says a colleague (in impeccable English).

Technology has played a huge part in improving standards of English in China. It has also made language-learning easier, more intuitive and more fun. The five-year-old daughter of a neighbour of mine speaks remarkable English, although she's entirely self-taught (she doesn't go to nursery and won't start school until next year). Her parents reasoned that if she were going to watch cartoons on DVD, she might as well watch English-language ones. And it has worked: she can express herself confidently and well. "The blue whale is the biggest animal in the whole wide world," she informed me solemnly the other day. Give her another 17 years of formal education and she'll be word-perfect.

So what does all this mean? Despite its legions of fluent English speakers, Anglophone call-centres are unlikely to be relocating from Mumbai to Shenzhen any time soon. Here, India has the advantages of history, of English's status as an official language and of its membership of the Indo-European language group. But if its broad workforce lacks the English-language ability that is one of India's colonial legacies,

China now has an expanding educated elite who are entirely at home in an English-speaking environment. That elite is bound to become more internationally visible; expect more Chinese leaders in multinational businesses in the near future.

And there may be an impact, too, on a different class of leader. China's rulers tend to emerge from engineering or scientific backgrounds. The current generation of Communist Party top brass received their educations in difficult times, often in periods in which Russian was preferred to English as the main foreign language. But within a decade or two, leaders will be drawn from a generation for which fluency in English is an essential component of a high-level education. Some will have received part of that education in the Anglosphere. The global implications of that could be considerable and positive, as US leaders find that they are dealing with people who, quite literally, speak their own language.

A Letter From China
31 July 2012
Justin Crozier

Chapter 11

Once bitten

Yi zhao bei she yao, shi nian pa jing shen.

So runs the Chinese saying: "Once bitten by a snake, you are frightened even by a rope"

Last week it was knots rather than rope that caused the alarm: specifically, the rate of knots at which teenage swimmer Ye Shiwen ate up London's Olympic pool in the 400-metre medley. After Ye knocked five seconds off her previous personal best and a second off the world record, the Western media took even less time to raise the spectre of doping, with US coach John Leonard describing her final splits as "just not right".

For Leonard and many other Western commentators, there was an obvious snake in the water: the systematic doping among Chinese swimmers in the 1990s. But those suspecting foul play often did so in contradictory ways. For the UK's Daily Mail, for example, Ye was reminiscent of the steroidal East German athletes of the 1970s, with "that same masculine, almost wall-like figure; the same impossibly wide shoulders and huge, rounded thighs; the same armchair-leg calves." For others, it was the fact that she was actually shorter and lighter than most of her rivals that raised suspicions. In any event, her tests came back clean.

Unsurprisingly, there has been a strong reaction here in China. The various weibo sites (Twitter equivalents) have been alive with indignation. "Haven't there been more Americans banned for doping?" enquired a typical netizen (indeed there have).

Chinese sports fans do have grounds for feeling aggrieved. Much attention has been drawn to the fact that Ye's final 50-metre split was faster than that of Ryan Lochte, the men's gold medallist in the same event. But it has since been pointed out that Rebecca

Adlington, the darling of British swimming, swam the final 50 metres of an 800-metre race even quicker last year (with no questions asked). And comparable improvements by other athletes over shorter distances at this Olympics attracted few suspicions.

On the other hand, given the chemical assistance that Chinese swimmers received in the past, it's unsurprising that suspicions have arisen. Indeed, the Chinese authorities recently suspended one of Ye's own teammates for doping. But claims that Ye has "come out of nowhere" hardly stand up (she was only the world champion in the 200-metre medley ...). And the assumption that China had or has a comprehensive state-sponsored doping programme equivalent to East Germany's seems to be wide of the mark.

That's not to say that there's nothing to raise eyebrows in the way that China produces its athletes. The Chinese team was led out by the legendary basketball star Yao Ming, who was virtually the product of eugenics: his father, himself an outstanding player, was paired with a female equivalent (although he was apparently allowed to refuse the first proposed match). The 7'6" result went on to be the tallest player in the NBA.

That was more than 30 years ago. These days, the recruitment of potential star athletes seems to have more to do with identifying talent than manufacturing it. So rather than prospective parents being paired off, the actual parents of promising child athletes are measured to assess the future size and shape of their offspring. And state talent scouts are alert for any signs of prodigious athletic potential; Ye Shiwen's enormous hands and feet drew attention when she was just seven years old. In this way, the Chinese authorities excel in harvesting the country's genetic outliers. And thanks to its huge population, China simply has more genetic outliers than any other country.

But the hothousing of these athletes in state-run sports academies is increasingly controversial. While sporting success remains a government obsession, there has been widespread criticism on the web of the way in which athletes have been isolated from their families. Reports that the diving gold Wu Minxia was kept unaware of her grandmother's death until after the competition have provoked outrage on the internet, as has news that weightlifting gold Lin Qingfeng hasn't seen his parents for more than six years. "Misshapen development of competitive sports" was one pithy comment on Sina Weibo. Meanwhile, two newspapers that criticised 17-year-old female weightlifter Zhou Jun for missing her ambitious target lifts in London issued retractions after coming under fire from Chinese microbloggers who considered the coverage unfair.

So while the state obsession with gold medals continues, public attitudes appear to be maturing. And there are other signs that China is developing a more mature relationship with sports. When the top-seeded Chinese badminton pair were disqualified from the women's doubles competition for playing to lose so that they might avoid an early meeting with their teammates, more than 47% of the respondents on a Sina.com poll thought that the decision was right as "the Olympic spirit should not be tarnished". And another 7% thought that the move was understandable out of concern for spectators. Only 27% objected to the ousting, with another 13% sympathising with the athletes on the grounds that it was their coach's decision. Even China's badminton superstar, Lin Dan, supported the disqualification.

Admittedly, "mature" might not be the word that first springs to mind when discussing Lin Dan, the greatest badminton player that the world has ever seen and China's sporting enfant terrible. Lin succeeded in defending his Olympic title at the weekend, adding his two gold medals to an already formidable roster of achievements: four world championships and five All-England championships among them.

Tattooed and seldom in possession of a shirt, Lin Dan has a similar profile in China to David Beckham in the UK. His face is ubiquitous on billboards and electronic hoardings, where he advertises everything from sports cars to chewing gum. "SuperDan," as he's known to his followers, is hardly the stereotypical Chinese automaton athlete. Indeed, he is alleged to have punched his coach four years ago and thrown a racquet at a line judge two years before that.

But while such behaviour is hardly to be commended, it is refreshing to see a Chinese sports celebrity enjoy the fruits of success – in this case millions of yuan from endorsements. This is a relatively recent trend, with Li Na, China's leading female tennis player, another trailblazer. Like Lin Dan, Li Na is both prominently tattooed and has sometimes been at odds with the state coaching system. In winning the freedom to work with a coach of her own choosing, along with the right to keep most of her tournament earnings, the former French Open champion has established herself as a successful sporting brand.

It remains to be seen how many Chinese athletes will be able to follow pioneers like Li Na and Lin Dan in reaping huge rewards from their sporting prowess. The mother of swimming gold medallist Sun Yang is said to be busy negotiating his right to monetise his success with the authorities who have reportedly spent 10 million yuan on his development. But we can be certain that their progress will be closely monitored by China's increasingly vocal netizens. Perhaps the most encouraging aspect of the various Olympic controversies is simply the fact that they've been widely debated in China.

And the debate has not been without humour, even over the snakey issue of doping. On her weibo account, Ye Shinwen thanked everyone for their support, "including the doubters in the Western media". And one netizen found somewhat hollow laughter in that abiding agony of the Chinese sports fan, the country's soccer performance: "If we really have these kick-ass drugs, why don't we give them to our football team?"

A Letter From China
6 August 2012
Justin Crozier

Chapter 12

Do you know what you are buying in China?

As I travel around the US and Europe, talking to investors about China, I find that most of them are underweight (a brave pension-fund manager told me he was overweight with 2% of his global fund in China!). I also found that a number of investors are invested in ETFs (Exchange-Traded Funds) as a defensive measure. Do you know what is in these ETFs?

The US-listed FXI aims to perform in line with the FTSE Xinhua 25 index and has a market cap of US$4.4 billion. If we analyse the make-up of this index today, we find that 53.4% is in financials. This heavy weighting is a function of the high profitability of the state-owned banks, which is due to the wide government-mandated spreads that they have enjoyed for some years, but which now seem to be coming under pressure (pace the last two asymmetric interest-rate cuts). For the rest of FTSE Xinhua 25, 26.2% is in commodities (mostly oil and coal) and 19.7% in telecom utilities. There are no consumer companies, nor any healthcare. In fact there is no representative from China's massive manufacturing base. In the real economy, privately owned companies now account for over 70% of GDP. In the FTSE Xinhua 25, using a broad interpretation, private enterprises represent just 7.8% of the index.

The iShares ETF listed in Hong Kong (2823 HK) is larger, with a market cap of HK$44.3 billion (US$5.7 billion). It aims to perform in line with an index of the largest 50 A-shares (after an expense ratio of 1.4%). With double the number of constituents, this index represents a broader range of industries: there is 11.9% in consumer stocks (three liquor companies, a car-maker and a retailer), and 6.8% in manufacturing companies, though still no healthcare or software. Sad to say, finance is even more dominant in the A50 index, representing 57.1% of the index. Telecom is much lower (just 1.5%) because of the absence of China Mobile and China Telecom, which are not listed in the domestic market. The exposure to the private sector is lifted to 20.2% (though half of this is ascribable to Ping An Insurance and Ping An Bank). One point to note about this ETF is that it is rapidly losing its premium (now just 2%) because of new A-share ETF launches, some based on CSI300 – a broader index.

Investing in futures or ETFs based on the Hang Seng China Enterprises index provides no escape. Only 3.8% of this index is privately owned companies (H-shares are nearly all state-owned enterprises). It has a 52.1% exposure to financials and the highest exposure to commodities (27.5%). However, there are two healthcare stocks – Weigao and Sinopharm.

Before leaving the subject of index composition, perhaps investors might want to have a look again at the venerable Hang Seng. Even in this bastion of free enterprise, slightly less than half the index is now non-state owned. The finance exposure (46.1%) is split fairly evenly between Hong Kong- and China-based institutions. The 11.7% property exposure is still mostly Hong Kong-based. With a high exposure to utilities (17.8%) it is perhaps the most "defensive" index. But exposure to China's consumers is just 9.8% – and still no healthcare or software...

A Letter From China
30 August 2012
Chris Ruffle

Chapter 13

Face value

You will probably be as surprised as I was to learn that the Miss World Competition still exists. And you might be just as surprised that the 2012 incarnation took place in the Inner Mongolian city of Ordos. That China won was less of a surprise. This, after all, is a country with a huge number of "outliers" in every category; it's not just in the Olympics that China is able to harness some remarkable talent. It's also a country that takes beauty very seriously indeed.

Appearances matter ... China's legendary "four great beauties", three of whom caused kingdoms to fall

Appearances matter in China. The country's ultra-competitive marriage market is only part of this. In fact, this is one area in which physical attractiveness may actually matter less than elsewhere, given the often stringent requirements regarding education, income and family. But where looks matter much more is in the jobs market.

Although there has been some progress in employment law, appearance-based discrimination has long been rife in China. It was only in 2004, for example, that the Hunan provincial government dropped its requirement that female civil servants should have "symmetrical breasts". Today, job adverts still commonly stipulate required physical characteristics that have little or nothing to do with the job. The most entrenched of these is height.

Many Chinese employers dictate "minimum heights" which job applicants must meet. Soldiers and the police are unsurprising examples, but lawyers? Foreign-office staff? And even air stewardesses, where, one would have thought, a maximum height would be more justified than a minimum. What explains this? Well, to some degree, it's a simple (though grossly unfair) sifting mechanism. Faced with a huge population – and thus huge numbers of applications for any job – employers see attractions in arbitrary measures to cut through swathes of applicants at a stroke.

And to some extent, China's obsession with height is perhaps less about appearance than keeping up appearances. The country wants tall diplomats, for example, to project a certain status – just as companies feel that tall employees lend them a certain amount of "face".

But for many Chinese people, height is an important component of attractiveness – and for women as well as men. Not too much, of course:

men generally don't want their partners to tower over them, although many of the (stereotypically Manchurian and thus long-limbed) ernai – mistresses – of middle-aged businessmen and officials do exactly that. But the received notion of Chinese beauty certainly includes height as a component. Indeed, desired heights are generally specified on online dating sites. Height also featured prominently in a recent survey of what mattered in a mate, with the proscribed range for women being between 160 and 170 cm – tall, but not too tall.

That must go some way to explaining the predominance of high heels on Chinese streets. Across the country's teeming cities, female footwear – whether casual or formal, though there is often little distinction here – is deployed to boost the wearer's height.

Keeping the sun off

The most important component of Chinese beauty, however, is skin: specifically pale skin. Skin-lightening creams are one of the biggest-selling types of Chinese cosmetics, with some selling for around 6,000 yuan (£60) for a pair of small bottles (which might last a month). As the saying goes, yi bai zhe bai chou: "a white skin can hide a hundred uglinesses".

This explains the ubiquity of parasols on sunny days in China. And their effects are obvious. Most Chinese tan fairly easily, which makes it easy to distinguish the parasol-wielding classes from those who labour in the sun – street cleaners, for example, or peasants. It's also remarkably easy to tell a young Chinese-American woman from a genuine Chinese native: the outdoor "glow" favoured in the West is, by and large, shunned over here.

Along with pale skin, lustrous black hair, oval faces, high nose bridges and "double" eyelids are highly prized aspects of female beauty. Most affluent Chinese women can maintain the first two fairly easily, but the shape and structure of the face are a different matter. Not that that stops those who can afford it from trying. Plastic surgery is booming in China – according to the Economist, it lags behind only the US and Brazil as the world leader in cosmetic procedures, and there's a thriving trade in trips to South Korea where high-quality surgery is thought to be more affordable. (There's no shortage of low-quality surgery in China, with many beauty salons offering eyelid jobs along with customary procedures).

Even among those who can afford the best surgeons, the results are often mixed. A number of TV presenters have startlingly round eyes that make them look like manga characters – or goldfish. And if you look around carefully in restaurants or shopping centres, there are plenty of lumpy nose bridges, the result of inexpert stuffing with silicon. And then there's leg-lengthening (and thus height-increasing) surgery too, which, though riskier, is also on the rise.

All of this is easily ascribed to the influence of the West. Many commentators assume that these women are trying to look more Western. I suspect the truth is somewhat different. Yes, many Chinese women want to be taller, paler, with higher nose bridges, larger eyes and double eyelids. That doesn't mean, however, that they're trying to turn Caucasian. If I look out of my window, I can see various hoardings advertising beauty products. All the models depicted conform to a clear standard of beauty, with porcelain skin, large, dark eyes and slim, willowy figures: but none would be mistaken for anything other than Asian.

Indeed, globally, the West's enthusiasm for tanning makes it the exception to the rule. A preference for paler skin, especially on women, can be dated back to Ancient Egypt at least. Egyptian paintings consistently show women with paler skin than men, a pattern that most cultures echoed until a sun tan became a status symbol in 20th-century Europe (as a sign that one could afford foreign holidays) and people put away their parasols.

That's not to say that the West has no influence. China's standards of beauty have changed markedly over the past century, and international influence may well have played a part in that. But I suspect that Japan and Korea have had a bigger impact than the West, given the obvious cultural and ethnic similarities. And the West has changed its own aesthetic ideal fairly markedly too. When the Chinese went in for footbinding, the West favoured waist-binding through corsetry (and even the surgical removal of ribs). Of course, footbinding persisted longer in China. When I climbed Mount Tai, one of China's sacred mountains, in 1998, there were a couple of old ladies more or less crawling up to reach the shrine, unable to walk properly on feet that had been maimed to meet the fashions of a vanished age.

Foot-binding provides some historical context for today's wave of self-mutilation, although it was never practised by the Hakka or the Manchus; Manchu women, prohibited from binding their feet, turned to high heels to get a similar effect. But perhaps the simplest and best explanation for the aesthetic goals that many Chinese women go to such lengths to pursue is not a comparison with China's past or with the West, but a universal truth: commodities rise in value when they're relatively scarce.

She's got the look ... Iparhan, the Qianlong Emperor's Uighur concubine

In this regard, I think the useful comparison from the West is blonde hair. Only a small minority of Westerners are naturally blonde, but many more choose to dye or bleach their hair to achieve an unusual appearance. In the same way, there are many people with naturally double-lidded eyes in China, although they are in the minority. And the same goes for high nose bridges. Incidentally, both were traditionally more common in the north of the country.

I wonder if that's significant. If you ask a Han Chinese person about Uighurs – the Turkic people of Xinjiang – you may hear many things, not all of them pleasant (in the eastern cities, Uighurs are often stereotyped as dope dealers and thieves). But you'll also almost always hear that "Uighur women are very beautiful". Unsurprisingly, many Uighurs have archetypically Turkic features – with high, hawk-like noses and double-lidded eyes.

In today's China, the Uighurs are often marginalised. But they frequently occupied a more prestigious position during the imperial era. Under Kublai Khan, for example, Uighurs and other Central Asians formed the second caste, behind the Mongols themselves; northern Chinese were third-class citizens and southern Chinese fourth. And in the subsequent Ming period, many officials and aristocrats of the second caste continued to occupy prominent roles. In the Qing period, the imperial concubine most celebrated for her beauty was Iparhan, the Uighur consort of the Qianlong emperor. A contemporary portrait shows the high nose and double-lidded eyes that are still prized today. Indeed, although shaved foreheads have gone out of fashion, Iparhan looks like she would fit right in on the hoardings outside my window. And earlier dynasties often relied on close links with Turkic warrior aristocrats of various stripes. So it may not be entirely fanciful to look for some legacy of this even in contemporary notions of good looks.

But whatever the origins of the preferred look, there's no doubting the cost and pain that many women will endure in their efforts to achieve it. The boom in cosmetic surgery in China must be in part simply a reflection of a global trend accelerated by improved technology and celebrity culture, and reflecting national anxieties and preferences. So while it's eyelids and noses in China, it's buttocks in Brazil and breasts and bellies in the US. Not that there isn't considerable cross-over:

near where I live, a buxom young lady bulges from a billboard with the English legend "Here comes miracle!". She's advertising breast-enhancement products, in this case, "natural" treatments rather than surgery. So some trends are universal.

Other causes are more China-specific. The job market is frequently cited as a factor in cosmetic surgery. The height-based restrictions I mentioned earlier are only one element here. One should never forget that China is an incredibly competitive place, given the pressures of population and the possibility of rapid advances in a boom time. So anything that provides an edge tends to be exploited to the full — hence all the extra-curricular education for which anxious parents are willing to pay. Even without China's sometimes rather backward hiring policies, an attractive candidate is likely to do better than a plainer one, all else being equal. The rush to go under the scalpel is just an acknowledgement that every little helps.

And there's another factor too. As prosperity rises, many young Chinese women find themselves with disproportionately higher disposable incomes. Single women still tend to live with their parents until they marry — and city-dwellers are marrying later. Saving to buy a flat is still seen as a potential husband's duty, so young women are more likely to have spare cash than their male counterparts. Add to that the narcissism fostered by the one-child policy, and it's easy to see why single girls feel that "they're worth it".

And here, as perhaps everywhere, the rise of celebrity culture has both encouraged the quest for perfection and served to make surgical inter-vention more acceptable. The role models here tend not to be those Chinese stars best known internationally. Indeed, a common com-plaint on China's lively, often ungracious blogosphere is that globally renowned ethnically Chinese actresses do not live up to the received standards of beauty. Lucy Liu, star of Ally McBeal and Charlie's Angels, is a frequent target of these ungallant remarks, as is Crouching Tiger, Hidden Dragon actress Zhang Ziyi, who is often hailed as one of the world's most beautiful people in the West. Even Gong Li, perhaps China's best-known actress, is denigrated: "too much like a queen and not enough like a princess", as a Beijing office worker told me. That may have something to do with her adoption of Singaporean citizenship; one feels that national pride is often an element here. Differing standards of beauty probably play a part too,

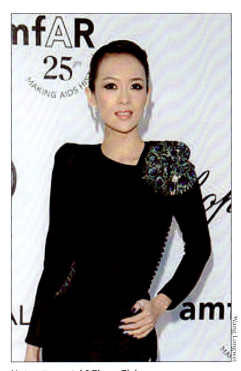

Not up to scratch? Zhang Ziyi

though; I've recently been told that "Westerners like Chinese stars with small eyes; we Chinese like our actresses with big eyes."

Differing criteria for measuring exotic looks used to be much in evidence in the Chinese advertising that used foreign models. In the 1990s and early 2000s, you could often see adverts with Western "models" who, in their home countries at least, would have been well advised to retain their day jobs. In those days, simply looking foreign was good enough. Here I can claim some personal experience. In 1998, a desperate recruiter offered to fly me from Beijing to Shanghai for a well-paid day's work as a catwalk model. At 5'8", a less-than-svelte thirteen stone and with all the postural elegance of the average chimpanzee, I felt obliged to decline. The opportunity, I fear, may never come again ...

A Letter From China
5 September 2012
Justin Crozier

Chapter 14

Sticker shock

Deciding how much pocket money to give a child is a surprisingly tricky business in China. It's also a pressing question. In the land of the single child, temptations for acquisitive children (and harried parents) are omnipresent. Wherever you look, there are toy stalls and toy shops, as well as toy-vendors prowling the streets to hawk their wares to sleeve-tugging little emperors. Even museums are in on the act: they typically boast not just a single shop with educational and improving toys, but multiple stalls piled high with plastic gewgaws.

Pocket money presents a potential solution: answering "I want …" with "Do you have enough?". And it might also, one would hope, teach a child the value of money. But just what is the value of money in China? And how much of it should a child receive each week?

That's where it gets difficult. Ten yuan? Twenty yuan? More? The rather detailed, but small, toy dinosaurs that you can buy in a Chinese branch of Toys'R'Us (a chain which, rather oddly, lacks any local competitor) sell for 55 yuan – about a third as much again as they cost in the UK – and surely too much to be a regular purchase for a small child. So 20 yuan (two pounds) would entail three weeks' saving – a reasonable goal, I thought – and would thus encourage thriftiness. But no.

The problem is that prices here are so elastic that there's something gratifying to be had for almost any sum. And children, being the covetous little devils that they are, quickly discover this. So all hope of saving goes out the window. Instead, kids end up scanning shelves for whatever affordable delights are on offer. At least it improves their arithmetic ...

Another lesson that's soon learned is that international products can't compete with their local rivals on price. Take Lego. Their "Hero Factory" robots sell for 99 yuan here – presenting a nice five-week saving target, I assumed. But I reckoned without the local brand, "Star Soldiers", which has established a considerable presence in the Shanghai Science & Technology Museum. These are much the same thing, but they come in a range of sizes (and thus prices) and are much cheaper: the smallest cost just 10 yuan, while the 15-yuan variants are satisfyingly complex. So any chances of saving for the more expensive originals is remote.

East meets West

And conventional Lego has its rivals too, in the form of the Sluban range, which makes tanks, spaceships and rather fetching ancient Asian warriors. I hesitate to say "Chinese warriors", because the Sluban products are apparently knock-offs of the Lego imitations produced by the Korean firm Oxford. It gets confusing. And it knocks the concept of pocket money as a lesson in thrift squarely on the head.

But it's not just in China's toyshops that prices are all over the place. There's no easy answer here to such simple questions as "what's the price of a beer?" and "how much is a cup of coffee?".

I've mentioned the staggering variation in beer prices before in these letters. You can buy a 600ml bottle for one or two yuan in a supermarket, and you might not pay much more than that in a cheap restaurant. In a Shanghai bar, a much smaller bottle will cost you at least 25 or 30 yuan, and foreign draft beers often cost 50 yuan or more. The most expensive beer I've had was in a German restaurant, at 80 yuan for 500mls, although it was admittedly a specialty brew made on the premises. But I'm told that in upmarket nightclubs, a beer can set you back 100 yuan or more. So the range we're looking at is one to one hundred, against perhaps one pound to five pounds in the UK (supermarket to flash bar).

Meanwhile, a coffee in Shanghai will typically set you back between 20 and 40 yuan. You can get cheaper takeaways, but generally, coffee is an expensive taste. In many of the Taiwanese-style restaurants that fill the food courts of China's shopping malls, a coffee can cost as much or more than a main course. It's as much a status symbol as it is a refreshment.

This illustrates one of the biggest challenges that China faces in the years ahead: the growing gap between the haves and the have-nots. It's a contrast that's starkest in the centres of big cities. The small plastic dinosaur at 55 yuan would buy you eleven cheap lunches from a street canteen: enough to feed a small building site or office. Or twenty-five sizeable bottles of beer, if you wished to throw a modest party. But you'd be lucky if it would buy you more than one sit-in cup of coffee.

Is one of these worth 25 of these?

But the dinosaur/beer equation reveals some other truths about today's China. First, kids are an expensive business – and much more so than in Western countries. Just as there are plenty of cheap toys to empty little heads of thoughts of fiscal restraint, there are lots of expensive baubles to attract acquisitive eyes. And toys are the least of it: even state schools and nurseries aren't free in China, and ambitious parents (i.e. most parents) face all kinds of other costs from early education centres, cram schools and other such aspirational excursions. It's no surprise that even though many urban Chinese, as single children themselves, are permitted to have a second child, most choose not to. It simply costs too much.

It also shows how much flexibility the relatively affluent have. If you can afford to buy your child a 55-yuan dinosaur, you can probably afford to spend the same on lunch. But equally, you could spend just 5 or 10 yuan on lunch. For those that are comfortable but cautious, there is ample scope to indulge in one of China's favourite habits: saving. Earlier this year, research by Lloyds TSB indicated that the average Chinese household has almost £20,000 in savings, against £9,000 in Germany and just £5,000 in the UK.

The reasons why the Chinese save almost half their income are well known: the lack of a social safety net and vivid memories of past upheavals. But there's another side to this too: people who save a lot can afford to make the occasional big purchase.

And in China, the most characteristic big purchase is some sort of status symbol. You see it all the time: humble earners who have nevertheless invested in luxury brands, whether handbags, watches, or gadgets – especially smartphones, tablet computers and MP3 players. You certainly see a higher density of iPods, iPads and iPhones on the Shanghai underground than you do on public transport in the West. And that's all the more remarkable when you consider that these gadgets cost just as much here as anywhere else (and so cut much deeper into local incomes). The reason? "Face". Branded goods – especially gadgets – are major status symbols in urban China. To have one is to be someone.

That brings us back to beer. My colleague Tony Wu put it very well: "In the West, beer's a staple; in China, beer IS sometimes like a Rolex". It's an excellent point. When the offices of Lujiazui disgorge their well-heeled workers onto the street on a Friday night, those workers aren't heading for a bar. They're heading home. The Chinese drink plenty of beer, but they drink it, in general, as an accompaniment to meals rather than on its own. So even today, China is singularly lacking in any sort of pub culture. There are plenty of bars, of course, but they're not generally places where people sit and quaff pint after pint over conversation – unless they're establishments that cater mainly to foreigners. But upmarket bars are, for many young, well-to-do Chinese, places to be seen. And if you're going to a flash bar, you want to drink a flash drink. Probably just the one – and it if it costs 100 yuan, so much the better.

There's a similar story with coffee. Many Chinese people won't touch the stuff, finding it too bitter or too powerful; I've met people who claim they can't sleep at night after having a small coffee in the morning. Those that do drink it tend not to drink it in the same quantities as their Western counterparts. So, in an acutely status-conscious country, an expensive Starbucks cup looks better than a cheaper domestic brand when you sweep into your office to start a day's work. For those that sit in, there's another aspect, too: space. But that will be the subject of my next letter.

In the meantime, I'm no further on in finding a solution to the pocket-money problem. If only children were more brand-conscious, they might find saving for quality brands more attractive. But the consequences in their teenage years would be both costly and horrendous ...

A Letter From China
23 September 2012
Justin Crozier

Chapter 15

In search of space

Stuck at the back of an endless queue, a would-be-shopper finds himself transformed into a snail. This is the Kafkaesque vision delivered in an ad for Yihaodian, one of China's booming online supermarkets.

It's a clever advert — and an interesting one. It captures a significant change among China's more affluent consumers, away from the traditional love of renao hustle and bustle and towards a less strenuous model. As many people in this crowded country get richer, they are increasingly in search of space.

Moving at a snail's pace

Online shopping is just one aspect of this, but it's a good indicator of the growing demand for convenience and comfort. It's certainly a fast-growing area: traditional retailers are suffering as consumers go directly to manufacturers' websites, to online supermarkets like Yihaodian and 360Buy, or to platforms such as Taobao ("China's eBay"). As Chinese department stores generally depend on several layers of buyers and agents to source their products, few compete with online retailers. Indeed, the Japanese department-store operator Uniqlo is the only major retailer in China that can offer the same prices online and offline.

But as the Yihaodian ad indicates, price is just part of the allure of online shopping. Avoiding the crowds is increasingly attractive to China's new middle classes. This is a significant development, for comfort and convenience have not traditionally been high priorities here. The best illustration of the extraordinary degree of discomfort that Chinese people were willing to tolerate used to come from train travel, particularly around the main national holidays in October and at the Chinese New Year. What was always so staggering was the sheer volume of stuff that people would lug with them onto the crowded train carriages: crates of peaches, apples and mandarins; boxes of dried fish; packets of vacuum-packed roast chicken and duck; and all manner of other delicacies piled high in astonishing bulk. Why, one wondered, were people willing to drag such loads from one major city to another? What was there that couldn't be picked up at the other end?

Some of this still goes on, but on major lines and at major stations, people are travelling lighter. The new generation of Chinese railway stations, like Beijing South or Shanghai Hongqiao, are unrecognisable from the chaotic hubs of the recent past. These vast, sleek hangars are more like airports than stations, with seats, shops and space. Passengers wait in the main hall until electronically summoned to the platform through automated gates that regulate the flow of travellers.

Spacious enough? Beijing South Railway Station

And the trains themselves are the equal of anything that the first world has to offer. I recently took a trip from Shanghai to Beijing. The last time I did this, in 2001, it took 17 hours. On today's high-speed train, it takes under five – as quick as traveling from Edinburgh to London. The carriages are clean and comfortable – so much so that the first-class carriages don't have much to improve upon.

Recently, though, I took a journey into the past, when I travelled from Shanghai to Hangzhou, the capital of Zhejiang province and renowned for the beauty of the West Lake, around which the old city was built. Zhejiang is China's wealthiest province, and Hangzhou is a delightful place, its verdant hills and vast expanses of water providing welcome relief from Shanghai's concrete jungle. In contrast to the frenetic metropolis, Hangzhou is calmer and more genteel: the taxi drivers even stop to let pedestrians cross the road. "This is civilisation," said one resident when I compared his home town to its vast neighbour.

But the charms of Hangzhou stop abruptly at the congested gates of its railway station, which is a turbulent hive of hawkers, beggars and harried travellers. It is the toilets that scream "Old China" most defiantly. The reek of urine seeps out into the corridors and is only partly disguised by the ranks of smokers puffing away under the "No Smoking" signs.

Perhaps unsurprisingly, Hangzhou Station's days as a civic embarrassment are numbered. Following an investment of some 10 billion yuan, a new station will open in a matter of months. This will be bigger than even Shanghai's rail stations and will doubtless match them for style and comfort. I doubt anyone will lament the passing of the old terminal.

There are other signs, too, of a greater appetite for breathing space. People are increasingly willing to pay for greater comfort, whether it be by taking taxis rather than public transport, paying three or four times more for a coffee to get a seat in a tranquil space (Starbucks have cornered the market here) or paying a premium at hospitals to get quicker service and greater privacy. Three hundred yuan (£30) per visit buys you more focused attention from a doctor, and it's a price that many are willing to pay.

Gyms are another bellwether. People in China's cities have embraced "lifestyle" gym-going at lunchtimes or after work. As a consequence, many gyms are grossly overcrowded. Some fitness chains have responded by offering a premium service at more tranquil locations. Ironically, these premium gyms are often less well equipped than their cheaper counterparts. But they do allow those who cough up the considerably higher fee (sometimes four times as much) to do their workouts without having to queue for machines or risk braining their neighbours with a barbell.

That most space-hungry of pastimes, golf, is growing in popularity too. Memberships of Shanghai golf clubs can cost between 200,000 and 1,000,000 yuan, but are regarded as good investments (they can be sold on to other aspiring players). There has also been a rise in private members' clubs. In Beijing and Shanghai, you can, if you have sufficiently deep pockets, shell out for the right to enjoy drinks and dining in opulent, elegant and above all spacious surroundings. Here, it's hard to disentangle conspicuous consumption from the desire for space, peace and quiet. It's clear, though, that you need the former to buy the latter.

That's the key point. For most of the past century, the Chinese have lived cheek by jowl and have become remarkably adept at putting up with each other's foibles. Visitors to the country often marvel at this. By Western standards, the Chinese can seem both extraordinarily unselfconscious and extraordinarily tolerant. Stroll through any park in the evening, and you'll find people practising taijiquan or qigong smack in the middle of narrow paths, playing musical instruments, performing shrill operas or singing karaoke with noisy electronic accompaniment – often within a few feet of each other. No one seems to mind. In the same way, people appear entirely unruffled by the jostling and shoving that public transport often entails.

But now that some can afford to remove themselves from the fray, it's becoming more apparent that hurly-burly may not be an automatic preference. As affluent Chinese seek space, they are starting to reshape the culture. They are also underscoring the divisions in this starkly unequal country. It will be interesting to see how this plays out in the years ahead.

A Letter From China
10 October 2012
Justin Crozier

Chapter 16

Taiwan recovers its mojo

Last weekend I attended a show of aboriginal dancing in Taroko Gorge in Eastern Taiwan. It would normally take several wild horses to drag me to such an event. However, a six-year-old child proved equally powerful, so there I was, clapping and stamping along with the best of them. At one point the lady MC, fetchingly attired in feathers and beads, asked the audience where it was from. Apart from the odd Australian and Englishman (sigh), the audience proved to be from Beijing, Shanghai

This too is Taiwan ...Taroko Gorge

and Shenyang. The MC gushingly welcomed "our compatriots" and thanked them effusively for their kind attendance. What was going on?

In the 1990s Taiwan lost its mojo. The main cause was the continuous and rapid economic growth of mainland China. Taiwan failed to exploit this growth through excruciating slowness in improving ties with Beijing. Obstacles continued to be put in the way of cross-strait investment long after such caution could be justified; direct flights across the straits were not allowed until July 2010, cross-strait currency clearance and settlement was only agreed last month, and we are still waiting for approval of the first Chinese corporate investment in a listed Taiwanese company. This was partly a failure of imagination by politicians still living in an era of Cold War paranoia. It was partly deliberate policy; the posting of the aboriginal greeting "Naruwan" over immigration at Taoyuan airport was, in hindsight, a sell signal as Chen Shuibian sought to tow the island further out to sea. The massive infrastructure build-out on the mainland coincided with the inability of Chen's minority government to pass budgets, meaning that Taiwan's shabby airports and road system started to compare poorly with the spanking new versions across the straits. From a position in the early 1990s, when an assignment to Shanghai was considered a hardship posting, Taiwan had become a country cousin, sidelined and irrelevant.

In the past week, travelling and meeting companies in Taipei, Taichung, Kaohsiung and Hualien, I noticed a change. In part this can be explained by the slowdown in China. This is not to say that Taiwan's economic growth is anything to boast about, but there are clear challenges to the investment-led economic model which has proved so successful for China in the past two decades. The leadership in Beijing has realised that hell-for-leather, unbalanced growth has its costs, environmental and otherwise. The regular flow of news from the mainland of food-safety scandals and disasters caused by faulty and corrupt building practices point to a major problem in ethics. With China's traditional religions long consigned to the dustbin of history, only a left-wing hard core still believes in Marxism, leaving nothing but the accumulation of money as a life goal. Religions that sprang up to fill this hole, such as

Falungong, have been ruthlessly suppressed. The government's half-hearted revival of Confucianism is a tacit concession of the problem.

Mainland tourists watch the changing of the guard at the Shrine to the Martyrs

Which brings me to the mainland Chinese tourists I met in Taroko Gorge, a beauty spot on the East Coast. The reaction of the visitors is generally positive, remarking on the friendliness and politeness of the Taiwanese. This has been reflected in digital media, such as in comments by China's most popular blogger, Han Han; he lost his phone in a taxi and was amazed when the driver returned the phone to his hotel within the hour and refused a reward. Taiwan has preserved traditional Chinese culture, with which is blended a strong admixture of Presbyterian Christianity. This makes navigating Taipei a different (more pleasant) experience compared with Shanghai. Even in physical terms, Taiwan has done a better job at preserving China's culture. The best examples of most Chinese art forms were preserved from the vandalism of the

Cultural Revolution under a mountain north of Taipei. The galleries of the Palace Museum are now packed every day with mainland tourists; the most popular exhibit is a jade cabbage, which boasts queues that I have only ever witnessed before outside the Tutankhamen exhibition at the British Museum. Seeing themselves through the prism of these visitors, the Taiwanese are coming to realise that they have much to offer.

Politics is also turning in Taiwan's favour. Democracy here has now settled down and there is less of the fist-fighting and furniture-throwing that characterised early sessions and which had their origin in the frustration of a powerless opposition. Now we have seen two peaceful transitions of power. This week I even heard the phrase, often used in the West but not before in Taiwan, "it doesn't really matter which party is in power". Heat has been taken out of the rivalry between native Taiwanese and the descendants of the waishengren who came over with Chiang Kai-shek, the Green and the Blue, partly, I

The jade cabbage in the Palace Museum

think, by the arrival of the Chinese tourists. Both sides have suddenly realised that they have far more in common with each other than they do with the noisy mainlanders being bussed around the sights. President Ma has also played a role with his newfound conversion to socialism (luxury tax, capital-gains tax, healthcare tax on savings) and bureaucratic approach to reform, which have alienated his one-time supporters and caused them to agree with his DPP critics. But at least the Taiwanese can voice such criticism of their leaders openly; on the mainland this is still undertaken only by the brave or foolish. And, for all the criticism of Ma, he has a universal reputation for being "clean", in contrast to the endemic corruption amongst mainland politicians, as highlighted by the ongoing Bo Xilai scandal. There was much admiring coverage of the last Taiwanese election in the mainland media. The joke on the mainland had a Taiwanese boasting how the super-efficient electronic voting system meant that results could be published by midnight on the day of the poll; the mainlander replies "That's nothing; here in China we can publish the result the day before the election."

Another aspect of Taiwan which the visitors admire is the ability to buy property freehold, rather than just "land-use rights". There is plenty of oral evidence of mainland property-buying here through third countries. The quality and variety of food in Taiwan is another draw. The night markets are particularly popular with tourists, and most seem to return carrying oolong tea and pineapple cakes.

In a reversal of trend, the newspapers now regularly feature articles where companies have decided to increase investment in Taiwan rather than China. The reason normally given is that wage and land-price inflation in China have narrowed the gap in costs between the mainland and China. Greater investor and intellectual-property protection in Taiwan, coupled with government incentives such as preferential industrial parks, together with increases in flexibility on use of foreign labour and reduced tariffs on imported equipment, have, in some managers' minds, tipped the balance. Clearly, if the mainland remains the end-market for their products, manufacturing locally still makes sense. But it seems that the long one-way flow of capital out to

China may reverse as Taiwanese capital and earnings, together with mainland capital, flows into Taiwan.

Taipei to Kaohsiung in just 96 minutes

Even Taiwan's infrastructure is starting to catch up, with big spending underway on roads and airports. I am composing this letter while sat on a smart train of Taiwan High Speed Railway (belatedly completed in 2007), being flicked between Taipei and Kaohsiung in just 96 minutes across a tangram of rice fields, fluorescently green with their third harvest of the year. Could it be that the Taiwanese are now starting to grasp the unique role they can play in the development of the region and are feeling more comfortable in their skins?

A Letter From China
10 October 2012
Chris Ruffle

Chapter 17

Gator aid

The two economic superpowers of the 21st century have many differences. But they have one thing in common: alligators. China and the US are the only two countries in the world to which alligators are native. While alligator mississippiensis inhabits the swamps of Louisiana and Florida, the lower stretches of the Yangtze are home to the world's only other extant species, alligator sinensis.

But US and Chinese attitudes to the creatures could not be more different. The American alligator is celebrated as a sporting mascot, a state symbol for Florida, Louisiana and Mississippi, and a longstanding feature of urban folklore (think of all those albino alligators that supposedly haunt the sewers of New York). After a period of endangerment in the 1970s, alligator mississippiensis is thriving again, with Louisiana and Florida each home to at least a million of the beasts, and another nine states home to more modest populations.

The Chinese alligator is far less feted. Indeed, it must be one of the least celebrated large predators anywhere in the world. Try as I might, I can find no representations of alligators anywhere in traditional Chinese art. The only reference that I've found remarks that they are never depicted.

I find that extraordinary. In my native Scotland, we put a great deal of effort into celebrating Loch Ness's non-existent aquatic reptile, so it's a little surprising that the Chinese make so little of the real thing. You do see alligators in Chinese zoos, though they're hardly star attractions. "Too ugly" seems to be the general sentiment. They're certainly in no danger of displacing the panda as China's favourite endangered species.

It's not even as if Chinese alligators are particularly dangerous. American alligators are much larger, attack about five people a year, and occasionally kill them. Chinese alligators rarely exceed six feet in length and offer no threat to adult humans. You might not hire them to do the babysitting, but they aren't generally aggressive. So what explains China's indifference to its alligators?

In part, the problem is that alligators lack any symbolic resonance in Chinese culture. Their fellow reptiles, the turtles, stand for longevity and so find themselves widely represented in Chinese painting and sculpture. Indeed, the Chinese language distinguishes between at least two types of turtle. Meanwhile, the alligator suffers the indignity of having to share a name with the crocodile: both are e yu in Chinese.

There was once a distinct term for alligator, tuo or tuo long ("alligator dragon"), but the character tuo is now utterly obscure. A tuo long does make an appearance in the Chinese classic novel Journey to the

West, where he, as a demonic nephew of the Dragon King of the West, captures two of the Monkey King's companions. But he is then arrested by his uncle. His captives are freed and he vanishes from literature.

Another rare term for alligators that does still have some currency is tu long. This has been literally – and somewhat breathlessly – translated by English-speaking conservationists as "earth dragon". But in fact the sense is closer to "mock dragon" or "low dragon"; "earth dragon" implies some sort of reverence for an elemental, chthonic creature, whereas tu has a negative connotation. A tu can is a "fake silkworm": the black cutworm, a moth larva that looks similar to a silkworm but produces no silk. And to describe someone as tu is usually to suggest that they are unfashionably dressed in a country-bumpkin sort of way.

Ironically, in the far-distant past, the alligator may have helped to inspire China's favourite mythical beast, the dragon. Certainly, there are similarities. Both are water-dwelling, scaly creatures. Both have paler scales on their bellies. Both have five-clawed fingers, and both have raised noses at the ends of their snouts. One particular type of aquatic dragon, the jiao or jiao long, is even glossed with crocodiles and alligators in certain ancient texts. But it is the dragon who gets all the glory; his real-world relative is largely forgotten.

More recently, though, the reasons for the alligator's decline have been economic rather than literary or aesthetic. Alligators are creatures of the wetlands. Unfortunately, so are rice farmers. In the 1950s and 1960s, huge amounts of wild wetland were reclaimed for rice farming. This both diminished the alligators' natural habitat and brought them into conflict with agricultural communities. While Chinese alligators pose little threat to humans, they are eager predators of livestock, especially ducks and chickens. On top of this, they dig burrows in river banks – or into the edges of paddy-fields, which can cause them to collapse. For those reasons, farmers have tended to regard alligators merely as pests.

As a consequence, there are now perhaps only one or two hundred Chinese alligators left in the wild. And, beset by the chemical dangers posed by rat poison and pesticides, few of those are thought to be breeding; indeed, the reptile's longevity may be flattering its numbers: alligators can live into their eighties, so a low replacement rate is not immediately apparent.

Happily, though, Chinese alligators do well in captivity. The Anhui Research Centre of Chinese Alligator Reproduction now has a thriving population of over ten thousand animals, and they breed successfully in both domestic and foreign zoos. There are plans to release a thousand into the wild in the coming years, assuming suitable habitat can be identified and safeguarded.

Unsurprisingly, alligators are sometimes eaten in China. I've eaten American alligator (inevitably, it tastes a bit like fish and a bit like chicken), but never the Chinese variety. A colleague has, but said that he found it disappointing. That's a shame: some conservationists see being eaten as one of the Chinese alligator's best hopes for long-term survival. Farmed alligators would be better than no alligators.

In the meantime, there are some encouraging signs. Various state institutions are involved in attempts to reintroduce alligator populations to the wild, with 15 hatchlings reported in 2009 after captive-bred specimens were released on a Yangtze island. Ironically, the hatchlings' parents were reared in an American zoo. Given China's hunger for

membership of exclusive clubs (the WTO for example), greater public
awareness of just how exclusive the alligator club is might help shore
up domestic efforts to protect these fabulous beasts.

A Letter From China
18 October 2012
Justin Crozier

Chapter 18

Sharp practice

The phonecall came out of the blue. Ni dezui liang ge nan ren: "You have insulted two men."

The accent was Manchurian. To Mrs Chen, a Beijing businesswoman, it conjured the stereotype of thuggishness associated with China's northeast. That, presumably, was the desired effect, as the message itself was blatantly thuggish: "You have until 10 pm today to pay compensation". And when Mrs Chen's one-year-old started crying, an extra layer of menace was added: "Or your family will get hurt."

Mrs Chen and her husband went straight to the police. There was reassurance there, at least. "You've got nothing to worry about," they were told. "You can register a complaint if you like, but it's just a con-trick. We get loads of these every week."

Sure enough, a search on Baidu.com (China's Google) showed that the same phrase had been used time and again. The call that Mrs Chen received was just a particularly nasty example of one of China's most widespread underground industries: scamming. The police were almost certainly correct that the threat was empty. The callers were hoping that their victims would pay up and ask questions later.

In Shanghai, Mr Zhao had an even more disturbing experience, when an anonymous caller warned that one of his legs would be cut off unless he paid up. Again, he found some reassurance when the police told him that they'd heard a lot of identical threats in recent months, but had yet to encounter any actual amputees.

In Taiwan, there is a nastier variant still: the kidnapping scam. This involves anonymous callers telling worried parents that their son or daughter has been kidnapped and that a ransom has to be paid. In fact, no abduction has taken place – but the scammers have obtained the son or daughter's phone number and have temporarily blocked the line. So when the worried parents call, they can't get through. This adds urgency to the proceedings – with the scammers hoping to rush their victims into paying up. The fact that there have been some high-profile kidnappings in Taiwan compounds the anxiety. I don't know whether this particular scheme has reached the Chinese mainland yet, but it's almost certain to arrive at some point.

That such scams are widespread suggests that they work. The call to Mrs Chen was just reconnaissance: had she proved susceptible, a time, a place and an amount would surely have followed. But she was doubtless just one of thousands of leads for these malevolent cold-callers.

Threats of violence are among the least savoury of China's telephone scams, but are just one aspect of a booming market in fear and gullibility. A police leaflet we received via my son's nursery outlines various different categories of swindles, including property, investment and insurance.

One thing is clear: in China, you shouldn't think of your phone number and address as private. I can speak from experience here. A few months ago, I bought a mobile phone from one of the state-owned telecom companies. In the Chinese fashion, I chose my own number (a tiresome and time-consuming process, as the first dozen or so combinations I came up with were already taken). The spam text messages began almost immediately – and certainly long before I had given the number out to anyone. Since then, I've received hundreds of text messages, of which perhaps only 20 or 30 were not adverts or scams. And there have been dozens of cold calls too. I've been offered property, surgery and any number of dubious qualifications. Either the number was passed on by someone in the telecom company, or – perhaps more likely – the spammers are hitting every conceivable combination of numbers by use of automation.

The net result is that text messaging is struggling to survive as a viable medium in China. Many people just don't bother with it: their inboxes are so clogged that it's not worth dredging it for genuine messages. I certainly don't: today, my inbox has over 60 unread messages.

And if the spam that follows registering a phone is bad enough, it gets far worse should you buy car insurance or property in any of the larger cities. Inevitably, your details are spirited to nefarious call-centres and marked as "high-income". You can then look forward to wholesale bombardment by the cold-callers.

Not all the spammers are scammers, of course. There are plenty of legitimate companies hoping to carve off a slice of your disposable income. Indeed, the hunger for "leads" is such that there is a thriving trade in phone numbers, emails and addresses. Rates apparently range from 0.1 yuan to 10 yuan per individual, depending on the level of detail and the likely level of income.

But even when legitimate businesses harvest these businesses, the means by which they do so are often deeply suspect – or are only one remove away from the seriously dodgy. Recruitment fairs are a case in point. While they ostensibly collect the CVs of jobseekers to put them in touch with potential employers, they often serve to provide scammers with a rich crop of potential targets and a wealth of detail on their lifestyles.

I have to say that most Chinese cold-callers aren't especially persistent. The impression is that they have such a mountain of leads to work through that they don't want to waste time if they don't immediately scent opportunity.

And whether the callers are peddling insurance, gym memberships or death threats, cold-calling is, in the end, a numbers game. They are dealing with "local" populations counted in the tens of millions, so their chances of finding susceptible listeners are always going to be decent if they have the grit and the temerity to keep plugging on. Good for telemarketers, if not for phone owners.

But even if you use your phone only with reluctance, it pays to keep an eye out for scam artists. Tourist spots in the big cities are haunted by "students" who aim to lure the unwary off to tea-tasting sessions:

sessions that prove inordinately expensive when the bill finally arrives. Heavies lurk in the shadows in case the victim protests. Variations involve attractive young women anxious to be taken for a drink or to proffer massage. And attractive young women are potential targets too: one common trick, which hinges on the victim's vanity, is an approach by the "talent scouts" of a model agency. This particular agency requires that the potential model put together a portfolio of photographs. These turn out to be at her own – substantial – expense.

All of this is perhaps the inevitable consequence of the breakneck speed with which China has embraced capitalism. A get-rich-quick society offers both high roads and low roads to lucre. It's easy to compare today's smoggy Chinese cities to Dickensian London. It's hardly a stretch, then, to see the scammers, con-men and extortionists, hunkered down with their headsets in clandestine call centres, as real-life counterparts of Fagin, Bill Sykes or Magwitch.

There's a crucial difference, though: Dickens' villains were operating outside a clear (Judaeo-Christian) ethical framework. China's scam-artists and shakedown merchants are not. A consequence of the country's traumatic 20th-century history was the dismantling of its traditional system of ethics. The replacement, the Communist selflessness epitomised by the apocryphal good soldier and model citizen Lei Feng, quickly withered. Today, many people are hungry for alternatives: witness the resurgence in religions new and old, as well as attempts to revive Confucianism. Others, however, are finding that the ethical void suits them just fine.

A Letter From China
25 October 2012
Justin Crozier

Chapter 19

Hungry ghosts

This week, the Christmas decorations went up on the walls of Super Brand Mall, a high-end shopping centre in Shanghai's financial district. China may be on course to be the world's largest Christian country by mid-century, but Christmas here is strictly commercial. Over the next couple of months, there will be lavish helpings of Santa hats, reindeer and Christmas trees in department-store windows.

A Halloween display on Shanghai's Nanjing Road

Christmas, and to a lesser extent, Halloween, are different. They have been so mercilessly commercialised in the West that there's a clear template to follow. For Christmas, that means creating a hunger for toys of all kinds. For Halloween, it means masks, skeletons, bats, witches' hats and plastic pumpkins.

Last night, my children went to a Halloween party at the "education centre" where my daughter is taken to classes, sing-alongs and playtimes. It's a rather peculiar institution, in some ways: the classes for one-year-olds seem a little like dog-training to me: the kids are gently encouraged to walk in straight lines, to build blocks in prescribed patterns and to clap rhythmically along with the teachers. But the sing-alongs and the soft-play area are fun, and the teachers don't particularly seem to mind that my daughter refuses to follow instructions to the letter.

The party, however, was not much fun. It looked the part: it was full of kids dressed as witches and ghosts, and the hall and the staff were appropriately decked out. But there was no ducking for apples, no games, no music, no food and no drink. Instead, the format was this: the children, bedecked in their spooky garb, were to sit neatly in rows, listen to questions and put their hands up to answer. Those who answered successfully would get a small prize. There were at least fifty children in the room, so a lot of sitting still was involved. And that was it. Parents were not allowed in, but had to watch the proceedings through the glass doors.

For a four-year-old and a twenty-month-old, this was all a bit much. Along with a few other refuseniks, they soon made their exit, and we felt no compulsion to force them to continue. But there was something as eerie as any ghost in the way that most of these very young children sat, patiently if not quietly, and waited for proceedings to unfold. I thought of the dog-training classes: evidently, they worked. Meanwhile, their parents diverted themselves with their smartphones and iPads.

Well, perhaps the prizes were worth the wait. We didn't stay to find out. In any case, that fifty children were all tricked out in witches' hats and skeleton masks shows the success of China's retailers in exploiting even this relatively minor date in the Western calendar. Certainly, the foreign festival is far more prominent on the mainland than China's native ghost-festival, Gui Yue, or "Ghost Month", when "hungry ghosts" wander the earth.

Indeed, in mainland China, the festival is virtually extinct – my mainland colleagues hadn't heard of it. It may survive in some rural areas, but it appears to have been a victim of the Cultural Revolution.

In other parts of the Sinosphere, however, the Hungry Ghost Festival is a major event. In Taiwan, the seventh lunar month starts with a ceremony during which temple gates are thrown open to mark the opening of the gates of Hell. As the month progresses, people prepare food and drink for the ghosts, and burn "Hell money" to provide these predatory revenants with more comfortable afterlives.

For the other months of the year, ghosts are simply "ghosts" (gui). But during Ghost Month, they are scrupulously referred to as hao xiong di ("good brothers"), to avoid causing offence to them. This echoes the former practice in the British Isles of referring to fairies (themselves sometimes believed to be spirits of the dead) as the "Good Folk" – essentially because they weren't good and were thought to be dangerous if angered.

And in Taiwan, people still believe that "hungry ghosts" pose risks to the living. It is considered a bad idea to buy a car or property during this period, or to get married. Children are warned against swimming or playing on beaches, where vengeful ghosts may be lurking to drown them. Surgery is another bad idea, as is walking alone after dark.

All this lasts until midnight on the last day of the lunar month, when the gates of Hell close and the living are able to return to normality.

It's a rich tradition, and one that is common to most Chinese communities outside the mainland. It would seem to me a pity if China continues to adopt the commercial aspects of Halloween rather than revive its own rich and strange ghostly heritage. But the retailers doing a roaring trade in witch hats and pumpkins on Shanghai's Nanjing Road might very well disagree.

A Letter From China
31 October 2012
Justin Crozier

Chapter 20

Nobel intentions

A friend was unequivocal: "I find his novels so disgusting: all that killing and skinning and blood."

It's fair to say that the award of this year's Nobel Prize in Literature to Mo Yan has caused mixed reactions in China. Debate on the weibo microblogs has been lively and has covered the merits of the award itself, China's attitude to international accolades, and even whether Mo should wear black tie or traditional Chinese dress to December's award ceremony in Stockholm.

Mo Yan

As far as domestic politics go, Mo Yan is a far less controversial choice than previous Chinese winners of the Nobel Prize. He is, after all, a member of the Communist Party. But he is also a subversive voice.

Most of his books have a strong satirical streak. And since winning the prize, Mo has said that he hopes that imprisoned Chinese dissidents, including fellow Nobel laureate Liu Xiaobo, will be released.

But the great concern of Chinese netizens is what the award of the prize to Mo Yan means. While many are pleased to see a Chinese writer recognised, others view the Nobel Committee's choice with suspicion. Why? The answer lies in Mo's frequently gruesome subject matter and his mockery of various aspects of China, both today and in the recent past. Among other things, his books deal with corrupt officials, greedy peasants and a whole host of grotesque characters and behaviour, including flaying, dismemberment and cannibalism. For many Chinese, these aren't pleasing topics, especially in the context of a Nobel Prize.

This is a familiar trope in China: the longstanding grumble that the West recognises only those Chinese artists who emphasise the darker aspects of the country's culture and history. The film director Zhang Yimou is a case in point. Before he started directing blockbusters (and Olympic ceremonies), Zhang specialised in dramas set in China's uncomfortably recent past. In particular, his collaboration with the actress Gong Li led to a series of films that won him international acclaim. Some of these were banned in China, though they proved popular both at home and abroad. Two, his directorial debut Red Sorghum and the later, lesser-known Happy Times, were based on Mo Yan's works.

But while Zhang won Oscar nominations for Ju Dou and Raise the Red Lantern, as well as a host of European prizes, even his domestic enthusiasts doubted the motives for the awards. Rather than seeing recognition of universal themes expertly handled (Ju Dou, for example, is a rural tragedy of which Thomas Hardy could be proud), they detect a celebration of all that is, or has been, wrong with China. Perversely, foreign institutions are seen to be snubbing China even as they acknowledge some of her artists. Today, some of the same suspicions attach themselves to Mo Yan's Nobel Prize. One current rumour is that Mo was rewarded for a veiled attack on China's one-child policy in his latest novel Frog.

To the foreign observer, this can seem simple paranoia. I sometimes point out that most Scots seem quite happy that Trainspotting, a dark picaresque about heroin addicts, was voted the best Scottish film ever; certainly, it shows a side of Edinburgh that the tourists probably miss. But there are other aspects to the mixed feelings produced by Mo and Zhang's recognition overseas. Chinese culture has a deep-seated dislike of washing dirty laundry in public. As the saying runs, jia chou bu ke wai yang ("Family ugliness should not be published"). Unsurprisingly, this is something that the government is keen to encourage: hence the eternal refrain of "no interference in China's sovereign affairs".

The same sensitivities apply even within China. The US-based Chinese detective writer Qiu Xiaolong has noted that translations of his books published in Shanghai (where they are set) are anonymised, with street names changed and Shanghai rechristened "H City". But the Beijing publishing house that has translated his more recent novels is happy to leave the Shanghai placenames intact: Shanghai, after all, is not Beijing, and fictional crimes taking place there don't tarnish the reputation of the capital.

Another factor is that a shackled press encourages people to become expert at inference and mistrustful of surface explanations. Detecting conspiracies is thus an unacknowledged national pastime in China. And it often leads to their detection where none exist. More generally, the ubiquity of propaganda can mean that everything is seen as propaganda.

Conversation with Chinese friends often reveals the ascribing of ulterior motives to all manner of phenomena, from schlocky Hollywood films like 300 ("whipping up anti-Iranian sentiment") to monitoring pollution from embassies ("a trick to embarrass China").

A "them and us" nationalism is part of it too. But it isn't simply a question of chauvinism, but rather of "face". Collective shame – whether on behalf of family, province or country – plays a significant role in the Chinese psyche. You see it in netizens' reactions to the videos of street brawls, drunken escapades and scatological outrages that are regularly posted on the weibo sites. "Foreigners will look down on Chinese even more after seeing this, especially if people from Hong Kong and Taiwan see" was a typical reaction to an incident in the last of these categories the other week.

"Mo Yan" is in fact a pen name that means "Don't speak" – the advice given to the young Guan Moye by his mother during the perilous period of the Cultural Revolution. While there's considerable pride in his achievements here, there's also a contradictory sense that perhaps he ought to have kept his mouth shut.

I confess to having read just one of Mo's novels, the rollicking Republic of Wine, which features cannibalism, a sexy lady truck driver and a scaly demon. Now, as much as I like those things (in books, at least), I admit to finding the novel rather hard work. Some of it was enjoyable, but I can't claim to remember much about the plot. But there was certainly a remarkable energy to the book, as well as some pointed satire of China's officialdom and corruption.

It's ironic, then, that Mo Yan's big win has already produced some comic sequels of official greed. Gaomi, his native county in Shandong province, has moved quickly to capitalise on his Nobel success. According to the Beijing News, plans are afoot for a "Mo Yan Cultural Experience Zone" in Pingan, the village in which the author lived for 20 years. The fact that Pingan natives no longer grow the crop that gave its name to Mo Yan's best-known novel is no obstacle: some local officials plan to pay farmers to plant the unprofitable red sorghum for appearances' sake.

Nobody should be surprised that local officials pounce on any opportunity exuding the faintest whiff of cash. Many years ago, I visited one of Shandong's older literary attractions, the Zibo Liaozhai City. This creaky theme park was built in tribute to the 17th-century master of supernatural tales, Pu Songling. The English Pu

Red sorghum: coming to a field near you?

scholar with whom I visited the park was the only other visitor. This at least made the decaying site appropriately creepy on a cold spring day. Inside the main building, darkened alcoves glowed with gaudy statues of the bull-headed and horse-headed guardians of the Buddhist Hell. Further in, a flying demon swooped unconvincingly overhead on a rickety wire. In a garden outside, a mangy menagerie of foxes paid tribute to Pu's hulijing, the immortal foxy ladies who tempt and corrupt various scholars and officials in the course of his stories.

It couldn't last, I thought. How wrong I was: almost 15 years on, it's still going, though with a higher admission fee. And some 300 years on, Pu's stories are going strong too. This year's biggest cinematic hit, Painted

Skin: The Resurrection, is both the highest-grossing Chinese film ever and the sequel to the 2008 adaptation of Pu's short story Hua Pi, or Painted Skin.

Whether Mo Yan's stories will enjoy similar longevity remains to be seen. But for the time being, sales of his books are booming. That's good news for Mo, and it's also good news for China. For a country with a high literacy rate (92%, and that despite the formidable hurdle of an ideographic writing system that takes years to learn) and a long literary tradition, China's reading habits often seem underdeveloped. A striking difference between the London Tube and the Shanghai Metro is that Shanghai's commuters rarely read books. For the most part, they watch films or TV programmes on iPhones or iPads, listen to music on headphones, or simply grab a few moments of standing rest. Some people do have e-readers, but you seldom see a paperback. Even then, most readers are devouring books on business administration, preparing for English-language tests or otherwise engaging in short-term self-advancement.

This picture is confirmed by a visit to any Chinese bookstore. There is plenty of literature, of course, a surprising amount of it foreign. But the shelves containing novels are inevitably dwarfed by overwhelming numbers of books devoted to the pragmatic and practical. Getting ahead trumps opening your mind.

The pattern is repeated among schoolchildren. In the West, a child's appetite for novels – especially novels written for adults – is a source of pride for the parents. Not so in China. Novels are a waste of time: children should be reading textbooks. This applies even when the textbooks are about novels; better to read the summary than the novel itself.

That's not to say that the world's oldest literary culture has vanished. Few novels can match the obsessive interest generated today by the 18th-century classic Hong Lou Meng (The Dream of the Red Chamber). But China's reading culture could certainly do with a shot in the arm. Happily, the Nobel Committee's recognition of Mo's work seems to be providing just that: after the award last month, bookshops and online stores experienced shortages as demand surged.

Another welcome aspect to the award is that in celebrating Mo Yan, China's government is publically embracing a critic – albeit one that works within the system. The China Daily claims that "Mo is currently the only Chinese author who has won the Nobel Prize in Literature", conveniently ignoring the 2000 laureate, Gao Xingjian, an exiled dissident who is now a French citizen. The Communist Party belatedly clasped Zhang Yimou to its bosom at a time when he was increasingly concerned with producing colourful, commercial but ultimately bland martial-arts epics such as Hero and House of Flying Daggers. But the prolific Mo Yan's body of work is too big and too popular to be tamed. Popular misgivings aside, it is surely encouraging that his pungent, inventive and shocking novels are enjoying official approval both at home and abroad.

A Letter From China
21 November 2012
Justin Crozier

Chapter 21

Sea of troubles

Last week, three news stories brought China's relationship with the outside world into focus. The first concerned the PRC's new passports and the provocative map they contain. The second was the successful landing of the first jet on the country's new aircraft carrier, the Liaoning. And the third was the People's Daily's straightfaced reporting of the Onion's satirical nomination of North Korea's Kim Jong-un as the world's sexiest man.

The last two provided China's microbloggers with a great deal of amusement. The expansive gestures made by the aircraft carrier's white-gloved deck crew have given rise to a new craze: Carrier Style, in which people strike the same pose in varied contexts and outfits. "Carrier Style" photographs have quickly become a weibo staple. And the People's Daily, in its po-faced quotation of the Onion, complete with a 50-slide online gallery of the Dear Leader, has provoked scorn and hilarity among China's netizens. "Actually, both of them are spoof websites," wrote one. The paper has since withdrawn the feature from its site.

There is significantly less humour attached to the passport controversy. This centres on the map of China inside the passport, which includes disputed territory on the Indian border, along with Taiwan and the

Hot spot: the South China Sea has long been contentious

"nine dashes." The area delineated by these dashes is at the heart of the current fuss. To the Vietnamese it is the "ox tongue". To the rest of the world, it is, more or less, the South China Sea.

The "nine dashes" on China's official maps outline around 90% of the South China Sea, with the "ox tongue" drooling down from the country's southernmost undisputed shores (those of the island of Hainan) to all but lick the coasts of Vietnam, Malaysia and the Philippines.

The "nine dashes" pose a number of difficulties under international law. Most obviously, they flout the notion – enshrined under the UN Convention on the Law of the Sea (UNCLOS), to which China is a signatory – that a country's exclusive economic zone extends only 200 miles from its coastline – and that this rule applies only to inhabited areas, not tidal islands. China does lay claim to both the Spratly and Paracel Islands, which lie within the huge area enclosed by the nine dashes, but these claims are disputed by Brunei, Malaysia, the Philippines, Taiwan and Vietnam (in the case of the Spratlys) and Taiwan and Vietnam (in the case of the Paracels).

That the "ox tongue" is outlined by a dotted, rather than solid, line adds to the confusion. China's claim, while boldly stated, remains somewhat ambiguous. It is not, for example, attempting to close the South China Sea to shipping – or even suggesting that it ever would. Just as well, as more than half the world's sea-freight passes through these waters.

So what exactly does China mean by the nine dashes? The Chinese authorities themselves don't seem entirely sure: a Wikileaks memo records a senior Chinese legal expert's admission in 2008 that he could not explain the basis for the claim.

The Nine Dashes

The assumption might be that the dashes represent some millennia-old imperial assertion, or perhaps a flexing of the muscles of Mao's China. But they seem, in fact, to be neither ancient nor an invention of the Chinese Communist Party. Instead, they appear to stem from the Kuomintang government of Chiang Kai-Shek. In 1947, the Kuomintang, then based in Chongqing, set out eleven dashes that defined their claim in the South China Sea.

After their victory on the mainland, the Communists took up the claim of the Nationalist foes that they had driven across the Formosa Strait. At some point thereafter, Zhou Enlai reduced the number of dashes to nine. And so they linger on today as an intractable problem, the durability of which is doubtless extended by the wealth of fish and, potentially, oil and gas to be found beneath the waves.

It is true, however, that China used to enjoy considerable domination of the South China Sea. In the 11th century, chroniclers noted that the Western Zhou emperors received a tribute of hawksbill turtles from the "barbarians" who dwelt there. And at various times, the whole of Vietnam was ruled by China. As the dominant regional power for millennia, China has plenty of historical precedents to fall back on, even if none of them quite explain the nine dashes.

But this, as with so many other territorial disputes, raises a key question: what exactly is China? One well-known answer came from the American sinologist Lucian Pye, who said that China is a "civilisation pretending to be a state". Foreign visitors to China often grow weary of hearing about "five thousand years of history". The notion of their country's age (and exceptionalism) is instilled into Chinese schoolchildren and the standard line is trotted out regularly.

But over those five thousand years there have been many different Chinas. As the celebrations every October remind us, the People's Republic of China was founded in 1949. The Republic of China (now reduced to Taiwan, though it continues to claim sovereignty over the mainland) was founded in 1911. The Qing Empire was founded in 1644, but it was ruled by Manchus, not Han Chinese. Before that, the Ming were Han Chinese, but they took over from the Yuan in 1368, and the Yuan were Mongols. And so on. Many of these Chinas had different capital cities and different aristocracies. None of them had the same borders.

And at times, parts of what had been or would be China were parts of other nations altogether. All of Mongolia was part of China during the Qing period; but just before the foundation of the Yuan dynasty, northern China was part of the Mongol khanate. And during the Yuan, the Han Chinese were third- and fourth-class citizens in their own country, beneath the Mongols and their Central Asian allies. And then there's the thorny issue of Tibet. Certainly, Tibet came under Chinese control during the Yuan and Qing periods (and of course in 1951). But in the seventh and eighth centuries, swathes of China were conquered by the warlike Tibetans.

All of this means that any contemporary Chinese claim based on history is likely to look at least a little contentious to the outside world. To the outsider, China's claims often seem to be as if the English were to claim that portion of France that they ruled under the Plantagenets. Certainly, the arguments are difficult to reconcile if everyone's claims are treated equally. If what was once Chinese must always be Chinese, what about what was once Mongolian, or once Vietnamese?

But from a Chinese viewpoint, these claims aren't equal. A strong undercurrent of nationalism in China sees the country's claims as paramount – and China's economic (and military) clout puts the issue beyond argument. That's where the Liaoning and its fighter jets come in.

It's worth noting, though, that it isn't just China that makes legally dubious claims in the South China Sea. Vietnam's claims are no less contentious, and the same applies to the Philippines. China has, rather slyly, offered to cooperate with both countries on developing the potential resources in the South China Sea – just so long as they acknowledge its sovereignty. The new passports – thousands of which will have to be stamped by officials of China's rivals – can be seen as a similarly sly attempt to force others to genuflect, symbolically at least. Vietnam, though, has responded by putting its visas on an insert rather than on the passport itself.

Ultimately, gesture politics, as exemplified by the passport and the nine dashes themselves, suit the Chinese government, which has to perform a tricky balancing act. The strength of nationalist feeling in China is hard to underestimate. Even the most mild-mannered and educated people can quickly become heated in discussions over these issues, and few of China's 1.4 billion citizens want to see their government back down in international disputes, whatever they think of its domestic policies. China's leadership thus finds itself in an awkward position, where any sign of "weakness" – no matter how sensible or pragmatic – can launch a myriad angry rants on the blogosphere, or even protests on the street.

China's rulers might also reflect that they have benefited in the past from persistently restating their claims. In the late 1990s, both Hong Kong and Macao returned to the motherland through patience and persistence rather than anything more dramatic; both were considerable coups for the Jiang/Zhu administration. Many Chinese hope for eventual reunification with Taiwan through the same patient means. So there's no motive for China to retreat from its claims in the South China Sea or elsewhere. In any case, climbdowns are embarrassing – as the People's Daily found to its cost last week.

A Letter From China
5 December 2012
Justin Crozier

Chapter 22

Religion, geomancy and superstition

Well, the world didn't come to an end on 21 December. Not that I was worried: I had, after all, received a helpful text from China Mobile telling me that the end of the world was "not worth believing in" and that cults have "dark agendas".

Not everyone got the message. In Qinghai and Guizhou provinces, hundreds of people were arrested for spreading rumours of impending apocalypse. A little draconian, one might reasonably think. What, after all, is the harm in a little millenarian doomsaying?

But one doesn't have to endorse the authorities' actions to see that they may have good reason for being wary of "cults" and their "dark agendas". A glance at China's history underscores that.

Those who were arrested last month seem to have been members of a Christian group known as the Church of the Almighty God, or Eastern Lightning (Dongfang Shandian). Among other things, they believe that Jesus has returned to the earth as a woman.

So far, so strange – and little cause for concern, you might think. But China has a history of trouble with outlandish Christian cults. In 1843 a failed civil servant called Hong Xiuquan announced that he was the younger brother of Jesus. By 1850, he had declared that the Manchu rulers of Qing China were evil demons and had embarked on a campaign to drive them from China. The result was the Taiping Tianguo, or "Kingdom of Heavenly Peace" and the 13-year war that it waged on the Qing Empire. This war cost the lives of at least 20 million, with some estimates placing the casualties twice as high.

A coin of the Kingdom of Heavenly Peace

So you can see why the current rulers of China might take millenarian cults seriously. Just as Hong Xiuquan cast the Qing as demons, the Church of Almighty God rails against the "Great Red Dragon": a red rag to a (Red) bull.

Nor was the Taiping the last supernatural-ly driven mass move-ment in China. The Boxer Rebellion of 1898–1901 has been described as "the last war in which magic was a major weapon". Pos-sessed by ancestral ghosts and believing themselves immune to bullets, the Boxers tore up railways, massacred missionaries and marched on Beijing in protest at the influence of foreigners in their country: foreign-ers who, some believed, sported the heads of animals. The resulting conflict split the Qing court into pro- and anti-Boxer factions, and led to the brutal occupation of Chinese cities by foreign armies.

And this was a conflict that finished in the 20th century – one that has only passed from living memory in recent decades. One driving force of both the Taiping and the Boxer rebellions was the number of discontented young men – not least those with no prospect of marriage; a problem exacerbated both by female infanticides among the poor and polygamy among the rich. It's a problem that still exists in China today, where selective abortions, especially in rural areas, have skewed the balance of the sexes so that there are many more young men than young women, and where the rich and powerful continue to keep ernai, or (unofficial) second wives. And it's not difficult to see how growing inequality could incline those who have missed out on China's boom times to hanker for some sort of apocalyptic reversal of fortunes.

Those explanations are mundane rather than supernatural. But is there something in China's culture that makes its people particularly susceptible to the preachings of cultists and wizards? As ever, it's always worth remembering that the sheer size of China's population multiplies its outliers considerably. If irrational beliefs are evenly distributed, for every nutter in the UK, you'd expect there to be twenty-odd in China. And if the Church of Scientology can claim 3.5 million members in the US alone, Eastern Lightning's million or so seems positively tame in comparison, given the respective populations of the countries involved.

Nevertheless, I suspect that Chinese culture does contain some peculiar vulnerabilities to irrational belief. This is an extremely superstitious country: my apartment block lacks both a 13th and a 14th floor, and it's not uncommon for tall buildings to miss out on every floor that ends in four: in Chinese, four, si, is a homophone for "death". Numerology, astrology and geomancy (feng shui) continue to be widely respected in China, and many people still consult the practitioners of these magical arts in pursuit of romantic or financial success.

And then there's the country's many religions. For all that the PRC is an officially atheist state, most Chinese are at least agnostic. And while Western agnosticism is essentially atheism (99% certainty that there are no gods, perhaps, with 1% left to entertain the possibility of supernatural beings), Chinese agnosticism tends to go the other way. As a result, a sort of pragmatic polytheism prevails. This is perhaps best viewed in terms of "opportunity cost". The average Chinese person might not actively believe in gods, spirits or demons, but the cost of appeasing them or seeking their favour is very low. From this perspective, it makes sense to visit the occasional temple or light the odd incense stick.

Burning incense at a temple in Yunnan

Equally, it's worth hedging your bets. Why propitiate only one set of gods if you can keep the whole lot of them happy? Even supposed monotheists get in on the act – so that nominal Christians (of which there are millions) will make pilgrimages to Buddhist or Daoist temples to pray for assistance on some specific matter or other.

Another element in China's embrace of the irrational must be its Confucian tradition. Above all, Confucian thought concerns itself with human relationships. Historically, this has led to an emphasis on human concerns rather than on the emphasis on non-sentient matter that science requires. It may seem strange at a time when Chinese students excel internationally in mathematics and science, but for centuries, Chinese scholarship has frowned on science. Successive revolutionary movements strove to reverse this, and the Communist Party has certainly done much to promote the hard sciences, but old habits die hard.

Nowhere is this clearer than in medicine. In private, some Chinese doctors despair of the support that traditional medicine receives from both people and state. While there are undoubtedly effective ingredients in traditional medicines (ephedrine was isolated from a Chinese herbal remedy, for example), the whole system is generally approached entirely uncritically – despite a lack of support from rigorous clinical trials. Experiments have shown, for example, that a fake acupuncture doctor is just as good as a real one – but placebo effects seem to be remarkably little understood here. Nor is there any shortage of people who will tell you that they know a practitioner of traditional medicine who will cure any ailment that you can care to think of – though they can rarely explain why these practitioners aren't reaping the rewards of introducing their miracle cures to the world.

Part of this is another Confucian strand – the respect in which authority figures, such as teachers and masters of traditional arts, are held. In many ways, this reverence for knowledge is a great thing and helps to explain China's success in education. But it can tend to discourage critical thought.

On the other hand, placebo effects can be real enough (at least in matters that are judged subjectively, such as pain or whether one feels better). So there may be advantages to having a nationwide conviction that harmless (though perhaps ineffective) remedies do actually work. But any such benefits have to be set against the undoubted harm that belief in traditional medicines do to the environment, and especially to endangered species. Consider the ti-

Chinese medicine: bad news for tigers

ger – a beast threatened by extinction largely because of the incessant appetite for bits and pieces of its body among believers in Chinese medicine. Not all of these believers are Chinese of course; Japan and Korea also have eager markets for contraband tiger parts, as do Malaysia and Singapore. But most of the tigers poached in India are ultimately destined for China.

When I ask friends and colleagues here whether they "believe in Chinese medicine", the answer is almost invariably "yes". That conviction does tend to waver a little if I ask if they really think that tiger-penis soup is an aphrodisiac, or if ingesting powdered tiger bone will actually make them healthier. Those aspects of traditional medicine are perhaps too obviously close to magic. But their faith in herbal medicine is generally unshakeable.

It's probable that there are some effective medicines lurking in the Chinese apothecary's cabinet. Besides ephedrine, the antimalarial drug artemisinin was isolated from a plant that had been used in Chinese medicine for over two thousand years. But the canon doubtless contains many ineffective and even harmful treatments too. Indeed, some traditional herbal remedies have been shown to be bad for the liver.

For believers, though, the proof is in the pudding. "I had a cold, but after taking Chinese medicine, I got better in just four or five days!" a friend told me (I've heard this line countless times). It almost felt rude to point out that I'd yet to contract a cold that didn't improve in four or five days. For people with visible, long-term medical conditions, daily encounters with the faithful can prove trying. A friend of mine in Beijing who suffers from psoriasis has had to develop a repertoire of blunt responses to the traditional-medicine adherents who approach him on the street to offer "cures".

Discussions with believers in traditional medicine tend to get a little circular. If Chinese medicine doesn't work, then it's because you haven't found a "real" practitioner. And you'll know if you find a real practitioner when the medicine works. But the system itself is never in doubt. Nor does it help that to many people, "Chinese medicine" exists in opposition to "Western" medicine. This opposition introduces elements of national pride, of "us versus them". And, in true Confucian fashion, a rhetorical appeal is usually made to tradition. If this system has been in use for thousands of years, it must be effective.

In this way, the power of authority – whether of teachers, gurus or antiquity – tends to overwhelm negative evidence. That's not to say that there aren't thousands of Chinese people who are as sceptical and informed as anyone else. China's many conservationists, for example, are infuriated by the claims made for parts of tigers and other endangered animals. But such is the respect accorded to tradition and to leaders that I doubt very much whether the Church of Almighty God's credibility will be hurt by the fact that the world failed to end last month.

A Letter From China
21 January 2013
Justin Crozier

Chapter 23

Big bangs

The bombardment began around eight o'clock in the evening. The far-off explosions stuttered out a succession of dull blasts, while those close by rattled the windows and flooded the rooms with gaudy light. Outside, the air was choked with smoke.

It was Chinese New Year.

Boom, boom, boom ...

Big bangs

Fireworks and firecrackers – the former light up the sky, the latter just go bang – provide the essential soundtrack to China's Spring Festival. So as the Year of the Snake approached, the evening exploded into raging cacophony that sustained itself for five hours. To venture outside was to be peppered with paper shrapnel.

And that was just the start. For days afterwards, the ritual was repeated. On the fourth day of the new year, the fireworks were out in force again. In Chinese, "four" is a homophone for "death", so clearing the devils and evil spirits requires an extra dose of explosions. I can say with certainty that this foreign devil was eager to escape.

Where we live, the displays were lavish, but entirely uncoordinated, with barrages of rockets being launched from neighbouring compounds at random. Only on the final night of the week, with work and school looming in the morning, did the gleeful pyromaniacs abandon their munitions. By the time that the daily commute resumed, the grooves in the pavement were inlaid with the scarlet detritus of firecrackers.

It wasn't just the pavements that were besmirched. During the last day of the Year of the Dragon, the Shanghai skies were remarkably free of pollution, with white clouds against blue over Pudong's Century Park. By midnight, iPhone pollution apps showed that the PM2.5 reading had spiked from under 50 to over 500: off the scale.

Nor was the smoke confined to the outside. Someone set off a battery of firecrackers on the landing of the 10th floor of our apartment building, filling the stairwell and the lift shafts with smoke. My neighbours went to remonstrate, but were met with shrugs. My father-in-law was outraged: "In Beijing, the people who did this would be arrested!"

There's a saying in China that "in Beijing you know you're governed; in Shanghai you know you're poor." For Shanghai residents, the city's affluence has taken the New Year celebrations to ludicrous levels: when even small children become entirely indifferent to fireworks, the displays have surely gone on long enough. God knows how much cash was burnt up in the lurid displays, but it must have been a hefty sum. And that's the problem: while the Chinese New Year might once have been celebrated with a noisy but brief barrage of fireworks, today's celebrants have the money, and thus the ammo, to keep up the bombardment for days.

The Chinese authorities have taken note. There are annual pleas and proscriptions; technically, fireworks aren't allowed in central Beijing for example. But these have had little effect. And every year there are fires, injuries and sometimes deaths from stray rockets or mishandled explosives.

Cameron Macqueen

More of the same ...

But there's more to the Spring Festival than relentless pyrotechnics. Above all, Chinese life centres on the family, and the family event of the year is the reunion dinner to celebrate the New Year. The menu varies across the country. In the north, crescent-shaped dumplings, jiaozi, are often the main dish; in Shanghai, a lavish meal is incomplete without babaofan, "eight-treasure rice". Fujianese and Taiwanese celebrants often resort to fo tao qiang, "Buddha jumps over the wall", a rich shark-fin and abalone soup.

These special foods are laden with symbolism as well as sauces. Jiaozi are said to resemble the gold ingots of the Ming era and so portend wealth. Shanghai's smooth and sweet babaofan signifies a painless year ahead. Fish, a key component of New Year dinners across the country, is a synonym for "surplus": both are yu in Mandarin. And the traditional niangao, or "sticky cake" sounds like "higher year".

In a country the size of China, family get-togethers entail not only a considerable effort in the kitchen, but an enormous amount of travel as well. Indeed, the Chunyun, or "Spring Festival travel", has been described as the largest annual migration on the planet – a migration that takes place in innumerable directions, as workers flood back to the rural heartlands while university students and graduates return to their home villages, towns and cities.

Modern China observes the solar calendar as well as the lunar one; 2013 was welcomed too, though in much more restrained fashion than the Year of the Snake. In a very real sense, though, the Spring Festival, with the colossal exodus that it entails, marks the big change. For millions of migrant workers, the holiday provides not only a family reunion but also a time to take stock of situations and weigh up options.

To the city-dweller, the changes are obvious. In the place where I buy my morning coffee, only one waitress remains from the four who were there before the holiday. The absentees are slowly being replaced. And the same pattern is repeated across Shanghai, in its restaurants, offices and shops, as incomers take up the places left by those who have gone to other establishments or to other cities altogether.

This time, the recruitment drive may take longer than usual. Already, Chinese newspapers are reporting a shortage of migrant labour, as workers have opted to stay at home after the holiday, or to seek their fortunes inland rather than take the traditional route to the coastal cities. As a consequence, the train stations of the cities swarm with recruiters brandishing leaflets promising decent salaries and good conditions.

The shortage may cause problems for urban businesses, like my local café. But for the migrant workers who form the human engine of China's economic miracle, higher wages and better conditions should be good news. Let's wish them a happy and prosperous Year of the Snake!

A Letter From China
18 February 2013
Justin Crozier

Chapter 24

Little and large

"Do you want me to help him up?" asked the young lady doing the belaying at the climbing wall at Shanghai Stadium.

I didn't. In his first rock-climbing sortie, my four-year-old was struggling determinedly with an overhang and had made little progress for about 10 minutes. "No, no," I said, "Let him keep trying."

My answer met with approval. "That's what foreign parents say. Chinese parents always want me to pull their children past the hard bits."

Now, I wasn't trying to engage in some sort of stiff-upper-lipped character-building. Rather, I wanted to eke out the possibilities for entertainment as long as possible. If this wall were conquered too easily, the more advanced ones might prove too difficult. Best to let him struggle at his own pace and save progress for subsequent visits.

Hanging around

I'd never have thought of taking a small child to a climbing wall in the UK. My son has loved climbing things since before he could walk, but playgrounds have usually catered to this need well enough. But here in China, they don't. Most seem to provide for only the most timid of small children. I have never, for example, seen a set of monkey bars in a Shanghai playground – and very few high or challenging climbing frames.

This fits with a general safety-first attitude among parents. Over the past year, my daughter, who recently turned two, has been gasped at by other parents for scaling structures meant for older children or by leaping into the ball pools in the soft-play areas that stud Shanghai's suburbs. She has also caused consternation among the attendants by going down slides headfirst: behaviour outlawed on safety grounds in China.

Of course, my daughter has a role model for adventurousness that most Chinese children lack: an older sibling. Inevitably, single children tend to be more cossetted than those in larger families. And in China, it's not just the parent, but the grandparents too, in the much-discussed 4-2-1 pyramid, with all the care and affection focused on the child. It's not hard to see that this discourages risk-taking and leads to a more pampered upbringing than in other countries. You sometimes see extraordinary manifestations of this. This weekend, a grandmother was hoarding all the balls for the air cannons at my local soft-play area, swatting away other children to save them for her grandchild. The fact that other kids were in tears left her unmoved. That sort of behaviour is hardly the norm in China (other parents were outraged), but it isn't unheard of. It's all part of the fierce competition for limited resources that characterises so much of contemporary Chinese life.

But quite apart from such extremes, grandparents everywhere are probably more doting and indulgent than parents. In China, the grandparents have traditionally done more child-raising than the parents. It's still fairly common here for small children to be dispatched to far-flung cities to be raised by their grandparents. Migrant workers often leave their offspring in the care of their parents when they seek work in the eastern cities or in infrastructure projects inland.

In many ways, China is a very child-friendly place. People don't seem to mind children being noisy or running around in restaurants or other shared places. Xiao pengyou ("little friends") are generally greeted with smiles and amusement. If you want a seat on the Shanghai or Beijing metros, tender years give you a better chance of being offered one than grey hairs (something my daughter quickly worked out for herself). And take a small child on a train in China and watch as she is showered with sweets. But when children get showered with sweets too often they get fat. China's swelling waistlines have been causing comment in the West for at least a couple of decades. It's easy to build an impression of a grossly pampered generation, waited on hand and foot as they trip over their own chins.

That picture is not entirely accurate. But there's certainly a widespread expectation here that small children should be plump. We have twice been told by our son's nursery that he is malnourished. A doctor at an international clinic rubbished this, pointing out that he was exactly the average weight for an American boy of his age (and I suspect that there is a fair quota of portly four-year-olds in the US). He certainly has no shortage of energy. The notion that children should be fat is not universal; none of my son's Chinese relatives worry about his weight except when he's jumping on them. But to many Chinese eyes, a lean child is worryingly thin.

A growing boy ...

For this reason, and in contrast to the pattern in Western countries, childhood obesity in China is predominantly an affliction of the affluent. Well-off Chinese families are happy to ply their children with sugary treats that poorer people can't afford. When my son's nursery class visited an organic farm, most of the parents fed their children with sweets throughout the duration of the coach journey and then, after the (healthy, organic) lunch, did the same on the way back.

There's another way in which China's childhood obesity follows a different pattern to that in the West. Principally, childhood obesity is associated with very small children in China, with rates declining among school-age children. There have been widely voiced fears about China's "obesity time bomb" for many years. In 1999, for example, the BBC reported that 20% of Beijing's children were obese. Fourteen years on, those children have grown up. But the young adults you see in the streets of Chinese cities don't appear particularly hefty.

Possibly, the harshness of the school curriculum whittles off the pounds. Or perhaps there's simply less time for eating when children have to spend long hours studying both in and out of school. There's certainly less time spent in the sweet-pushing company of grandparents. Whatever the reason, the visual evidence suggests that not all of China's podgy infants grow up into podgy adults.

Many of them do, of course. While adult obesity in China may not yet be on the scale that you might expect from media reports, it's a significant problem and one that may pose an even greater threat to health than in the West. Certainly, there seems to be a higher risk of diabetes among overweight Chinese adults. Personal experience tends to confirm this: I know many more diabetic people in China than I do in Britain. And indeed, China's rate of type-2 diabetes is similar to that of the US – and almost twice as high as that of the UK. The explanation of this appears to be genetic, reflecting a tendency among East Asians to carry more abdominal fat when overweight.

During the winter months, many Chinese children look overweight even if they aren't. Thick, long underwear is ubiquitous in China, and staying warm is an overriding parental (and grandparental) concern. Oddly, it's also a concern that is just as pronounced in Shanghai (damp, though not especially cold in the winter) as in Beijing (where sub-zero temperatures are the norm).

But it's not just in winter that children are warmly wrapped. It's only when the scorching summer months arrive that Chinese parents and grandparents seem to stop worrying about their offspring getting cold. An exposed stomach is seen as particularly dangerous; and giving a child cold water to drink causes no end of alarm. But being snugly dressed all the time means that the body burns fewer calories, as it doesn't have to expend as much energy to keep warm. Overdressing and overfeeding can thus conspire to produce fatter, less athletic kids.

So, as their elders make the most of their newfound affluence, some of China's children get spoiled and fat in the meantime. At the root of all of this is the one-child policy. It's now well into its fourth decade and may be on its last legs. Some expect the new administration to take steps to end the demographic experiment that overshadowed life in urban China since 1979. But it's unlikely that any relaxation of the restrictions will have a dramatic effect. Couples who are themselves only children are already allowed to have a second child, which covers most people in their twenties and early thirties. The overwhelming majority choose not to.

That's unsurprising. It's well documented that as a society enjoys greater wealth and higher levels of education, it tends to produce fewer children. Japan is the obvious example here. In China, though, this tendency appears to have been exaggerated by the one-child policy, not only because the strictures still apply to some, but because thirty-three years of one-child families has established a very powerful social norm. On top of that, the costs associated with bringing up two children are often prohibitive. This is in part a symptom of the one-child policy; the same pressures that drive families to spoil and cosset their children have led to a thriving industry of expensive educational and entertainment extras. Increasingly, these are de rigeur for China's urban middle classes. So, ironically, just as China may be starting to relax its prohibition on second children in urban families, rising costs and higher standards of living are conspiring to keep the birth rate low.

The demographic "turning curve" is huge, so there is very little that can be done to avert the dramatic ageing that awaits the Chinese populace. Today's "little emperors" face an awkward future in several respects. Above all, it is one that will be defined by relentless competition. Not only must they compete with their own age group for the limited pool of school and university places, good jobs and spouses (China has around six male children for every five girls; selective abortions, especially in the countryside, have sown the seeds of a demographic trauma), but they must also face up to supporting at least two generations of their elders.

To compound this, Chinese people are living longer. Shanghai's life expectancy already exceeds that of the US, so grandparents and even great-grandparents will be around for a long time to come. And so the 4-2-1 will be reversed, with the flow of goods and services, and – especially – time and effort, flowing the other way. It will be a heavy burden for the little emperors to bear. Though one might bewail the cossetting that cushions their early years, one can hardly begrudge them a period of comfort. The parents and grandparents who help kids up the climbing wall today, after all, will require plenty of help themselves as they negotiate the obstacles of senescence in the decades ahead.

A Letter From China
27 March 2013
Justin Crozier

Chapter 25

Peculiar knights-errant

The liveliest discussion I have ever witnessed in the Open Door office wasn't a heated debate over the fundamentals of an obscure A-share-listed company, or an attempt to predict the next turn in Chinese government policy. Nor did it concern football, fashion or food. Instead, it arose when I asked my Chinese colleagues whether they liked wuxia.

Wuxia, which translates roughly as "martial heroism", is the Chinese genre – literary, televisual and cinematic – of martial-arts adventure. It's the province of spinning kicks, dazzling swordplay and impossible feats, with a generous side-order of chivalry and romance. And it's very, very popular: every last one of my Chinese and Taiwanese colleagues was an enthusiast. There was no disagreement in the discussion that followed my question, but rather an outpouring of glee and nostalgia. Laptops were downed and reminiscences flowed.

Both Taiwanese and mainlanders remembered the first television shows based on the genre in the 1980s; both described the streets emptying as people crowded round the few available televisions to devour the broadcasts. In 1982, I was told, some 70% of Taiwan's population watched the dramatization of Jin Yong's novel Demi-Gods and Semi-Devils. My colleague Warren rewarded himself with a new Jin Yong novel every time he passed a school or university exam – and then read it non-stop until he finished.

Part of the allure of the genre is that it has frequently been forbidden fruit. The term wuxia is younger than the tradition. Though the genre's roots stretch at least as far back as the great Chinese classic The Outlaws of the Marsh (aka The Water Margin), it coalesced as a distinct literary mode in the early 20th century, with its name borrowed from the Japanese bukyo, which is written using the same characters. And it attracted almost instant disapproval. It's not hard to see why: wuxia typically features incorruptible martial artists struggling against all-too-corruptible officials. This gives it an inherently anti-authoritarian streak, to which few Chinese rulers have warmed. The newly identified genre was soon under attack for being subversive, for being anti-Confucian and for promoting interest in the supernatural. The Republic of China outlawed it at several points, and the People's Republic followed suit.

Indeed, until 1980, wuxia was banned on the Chinese mainland and heavily censored in Taiwan. Only in Hong Kong was it free to flourish, both on the page and on the screen. Some of my colleagues could remember the passing round of clandestine copies of books by the Hong Kong-based wuxia novelist Jin Yong, which people would copy out by hand (an early example of how restrictions on entertainment engenders a lax attitude to intellectual property: see also our letter Pirates at Bay).

As my colleagues' enthusiasm indicates, the wuxia tradition exerts a strong grip on the Chinese imagination. It seeps into Chinese historical films of all stripes, to the extent that it often seems as if film directors are incapable of shooting a historical battle scene without acrobatic halberdiers and pirouetting swordsmen. Indeed, the wuxia film is almost as old as Chinese cinema itself. The first wuxia film, The Burning of Red Lotus Temple, was released in 1928. It's a mere 27 hours long and is an adaptation of one of the first modern wuxia novels, Xiang Kairan's 1920s work The Peculiar Knights-Errant of the Jianghu. The title, it's fair to say, works better in Chinese.

The jianghu is a concept peculiar to the genre. Literally, it means "river lake", and it describes the typical setting of a wuxia novel. Beyond that, though, it's a little hard to define. Perhaps the closest concept in Western tradition is the idea of the "greenwood" – a place where the law of the land does not hold and noble outlaws can live beyond the reach of the (doubtless corrupt) authorities. Most importantly, the jianghu can be a sort of timeless never-land within a historical setting that is only very loosely defined. For while some wuxia novels take place in specific historical contexts, many have a setting best described as "long, long ago" or even "once upon a time". The related concept of wulin is slightly more specific, referring to a circle or society of martial artists. This is generally the community from which the protagonists of the stories spring.

For the Chinese audience, wuxia is clearly a potent blend. For Westerners, though, its appeal can be a little hard to grasp. There isn't really an equivalent genre in the West. Sword and sorcery might come close in some ways, but has nothing like the mainstream (and unisex) appeal of the novels of Jin Yong or Wang Dulu. There might be a certain parallel with the works of Tolkien, in the conjuring of a past that never was. And the Western genre has similarities too, in the way that it uses archetypes (white hats and black hats) and mythologises gunplay just as wuxia celebrates unlikely feats of hand-to-hand combat. The Wild West also provides a kind of "blank canvas" setting in the same way that the jianghu does, and Westerns often have similar themes of honour and revenge.

Such parallels haven't helped the genre to transcend its Chinese roots, though. A visit to Shanghai's main Foreign Language Bookstore on Fuzhou Road underscores the limited appeal of wuxia to an English-speaking audience. The bookstore, which extends over four large floors, gives you a little bit of the old PRC, mainly in the form of the resolutely unsmiling cashiers. Away from the tills, service is much friendlier. The uniformed doormen are cheerful, the helpdesk staff helpful, and if the saleswomen pushing Chinese language-learning software are a little pushy, they're also charming with it.

The ground floor, which is devoted to fiction, offers a fair bit of Chinese literature in translation. There are various editions of the four great Chinese novelists (Three Kingdoms, Journey to the West, The Outlaws of the Marsh and The Dream of the Red Chamber), along with 20th-century writers like Lu Xun and Zhang Ailing. But there is not a single wuxia novel to be seen. Cross Fuzhou Road to any of the Chinese-language bookstores that line the street and you'll find shelf after shelf of novels by Wang Dulu, Gu Long and Jin Yong, as well as many others. Some contemporary novels add sci-fi elements such as time travel to the tried and tested recipe of swordplay and romance, while others stick to the traditional formula. But they all remain stubbornly rooted in the cultural soil of their native land.

It's not that there haven't been translations. You can pick up the odd Jin Yong or Gu Long novel on Amazon. But given the dozens of works that each author has produced, pickings are meagre. Translated into English, the titles tend towards the unwieldy (Fox Volant of the Snowy Mountain, anyone?). And I suspect that the plots, with their tropes of honour, mistaken identity, magical weapons and invincible martial artists, can prove a little hard to swallow for Western readers who haven't been reared on them.

The one big crossover success, of course, was Ang Lee's 2000 film, the Oscar-winning Crouching Tiger, Hidden Dragon. But that film's international success, along with the brief flurry of wuxia epics that followed it on global release (Zhang Yimou's Hero and House of Flying Daggers), underscores just how limited the genre's reach is. Very few of the Western viewers who enjoyed Crouching Tiger know that it was based on a novel (published in 1941 by Wang Dulu) or that the book was the fourth in a series of five (the Crane-Iron series). And none of the high-profile wuxia films that followed had anything like the same international impact.

Crouching Tiger showcases many of the wuxia genre's traits. There is furious action, much of it hinging on specific martial-arts techniques, such as the Wudang school of swordplay or the Nine Yin White Bone Claw. And there is romance, typically star-crossed, frustrated or tragic. Lovers wait to be reunited for decades; or never speak to each other until it's too late; or jump off mountains to be together in the afterlife. It is, I think, these romantic elements that are the biggest impediment to winning over cynical Western audiences.

Nevertheless, one can detect an increasing influence of wuxia films in Western cinema. Stylised, acrobatic violence is no longer the preserve of films made in Asia. There are overt homages in the movies of Quentin Tarantino, for example, and the Yoda of the Star Wars films

is the genre's archetypal shifu, or master: a hermit who can bestow upon the hero magical martial prowess. The Matrix films are another obvious example. And the wirework that so characterises wuxia has even found its way into Peter Jackson's Lord of the Rings and Hobbit films – most notably in the incongruous kung-fu elves who appear in The Desolation of Smaug. Western audiences may not have much of an appetite for wuxia plots, but they're happy to lap up wuxia action. And if the Peculiar Knights-Errant can make it to Middle Earth, I suspect that we'll be seeing a whole lot more of their acrobatics in Hollywood films, as studios play to the ever-more important Chinese market.

A Letter From China
2 April 2013
Justin Crozier

Chapter 26

Park life

More than a month after the Spring Festival, winter finally gave up the ghost at the weekend. A freezing and blustery Saturday gave way to sunshine – perhaps not exactly glorious, as it filtered through a light smog, but certainly bright enough to make a visit to Shanghai's Century Park a pleasure.

For the past couple of months, the park has doubled its entrance fee, from 10 yuan to 20. The reason is blossom. The park's plum trees are in full bloom, and the pink and white flowers certainly seem to earn their keep, judging by the crowds they draw. Bright-yellow rapeseed also enlivens the scene, and there are colourful birds in the trees.

When the sun is out in any of China's larger parks, one would be forgiven for thinking that the Occupy movement has reached the PRC. Tents dot the lawns, as if an army of protesters has settled in for the long term. But no one sleeps in these tents, unless they doze off: camping, Chinese-style, is for the daytime only.

It's initially a little mystifying: why pitch a tent in a park, when you can roll out a mat or simply sit on the grass? But as one Chinese friend said to me, where else can you pitch a tent in Shanghai? The city's urban sprawl gives

Bloomin' heck! Visitors admire the blossom in Shanghai's Century Park

way to precious little open ground before it runs into other conurbations, and what land there is is flat and intensively farmed. The same is not true of all Chinese cities, of course: in Beijing, there are hills and mountains where urbanites can escape the choking smog and enjoy some genuinely wild hiking. But it's not camping-friendly terrain, for the most part, and you have to carry a lot of drinking water in the summer.

If you live in Shanghai and you hanker for the great outdoors, though, the park is pretty much the best you can do. Outdoor clothing and equipment is in great vogue in Shanghai, judging by the weekend crowds at the French chain Decathlon, even if most of it is used only in landscaped urban surroundings. In the heat of the summer, however, a tent provides welcome shade, so it's not all about wistful thoughts of the far-off wilds.

"Camping" is not the only diversion on offer in Century Park. In some places, there are signs prohibiting the flying of kites, but these are cheerfully disregarded. Frisbees are thrown, footballs are kicked, and if you want to pass around a rugby ball, you can be sure of people willing to give the curious ganlanqiu ("olive ball") a go. It makes for a pleasant afternoon.

Oddly, although there is a funfair with rides, there's only a tiny children's playground – a single low-level plastic climbing frame with dirty and broken slides. I suspect that the one-child policy explains this: it's easy enough to take one child on a fairground ride, and few Chinese parents have to contend with marshalling two or more urchins into some sort of semi-constructive activity. According to my colleagues, fear of lawsuits from parents of injured children militates against the construction of the sort of large-scale adventure playground that you'd expect in a Western park of comparable size.

Occupy Shanghai?

There are some interesting rock formations; climbing is forbidden, but no one seems to enforce the prohibition. There is also boating on the artificial lake at the western end, and on the canals that run through the park. And both children and adults shoot by on scooters, bicycles and rollerblades.

Shanghai's other parks tend to be noisier places, with amateur opera groups, singers performing karaoke for crowds, and assorted buskers – often all well within earshot of each other. On my last visit to Zhongshan Park, a troupe of burly drag queens was in full falsetto voice, much to the amusement of their audience.

On most sunny days, the paths of Century Park are crowded, not only with people but also with the tandems and pedicabs that you can rent to take in its 140 hectares at a greater lick. Taking a stroll can thus be rather fraught, as the drivers of the vehicles do their best to swerve past pedestrians, but you can at least escape to the lawns. Century Park permits its visitors to walk on the grass, probably by dint of its entry fee; many other Chinese parks – which are generally free to enter – forbid the practice in an effort to keep the turf from being trampled bare.

This Sunday, however, was quiet. It wasn't fear of bird flu that kept the crowds from the park: no one wore a face-mask or paid any heed to the pigeons and azure-winged magpies wheeling overhead. Rather, 7 April was a working day for most people – despite being a Sunday.

This is a curious feature of Chinese working life. When a holiday falls close to a weekend, as did last Thursday's Tomb-Sweeping Day, the authorities shift the weekend so that it joins up with the extra day off.

So, with Thursday a holiday, Friday became part of the weekend and Sunday became a working day – so that a three-day week is followed by a six-day one. The rationale is that a block of time off allows people greater freedom to travel.

In the case of the Tomb-Sweeping Holiday, or Qingming Jie, huge numbers of people travel to where their great-grandparents, grandparents or parents are buried. Here, they clear the graves of weeds, burn incense and offer comforts for the afterlife, such as alcohol, tea and paper goods. As well as the filial piety that is the mainstay of Confucian belief, there's an element of Daoist self-interest here too: the spirits of one's deceased ancestors are traditionally believed to have the power to improve one's own life if treated with due respect. Given that many Chinese find themselves living hundreds or thousands of miles from their hometowns, the fusion of holiday and weekend proves helpful.

The Tomb-Sweeping Holiday was one of three traditional holidays restored to the official calendar in 2008, along with the Dragon Boat Festival and

Flying high: a kite over Century Park

the Mid-Autumn Festival. This year, small cars were exempted from toll-road charges, so more graves, one presumes, were swept.

You could see this as just one of the ways in which the tendrils of traditional Chinese culture continue to creep through the cracks in the Communist edifice. But on a sunny day, under blue skies (albeit fringed by grey horizons), there was no need to overthink things. Those lucky enough to be off work on Sunday could simply relish the pleasures of an uncrowded park.

A Letter From China
8 April 2013
Justin Crozier

Chapter 27

Rain, rain, come again

For most of last week it rained in Shanghai; a heavy, relentless downpour that soaked shoes and turned gutters into rivers. When it rains, the few cyclists and pedicart drivers on the streets sport neon-hued plastic capes, and taxis become impossible to find. At the automatic doors of the more upmarket office blocks and shopping malls, staff handed out polythene scabbards to anyone carrying an umbrella, the aim, presumably, to prevent the smooth floors of the buildings becoming slick with spilled water.

The almost monsoonal downpour did, however, have one very welcome effect: it cleared the skies of dust. While the rain hammered down, Shanghai's PM2.5 reading (for the smaller and more dangerous particles) sank as low as 30: a figure that would be acceptable in a Western city. At the weekend, I played touch rugby out at the Shanghai RFC sports ground, where smokestacks loom in the background and an afternoon's exertions typically leave one with an unpleasant velvety coating on the tongue. Last Saturday, however, the wet, damp air was wonderfully clean. Playing in a fresh-air downpour was far preferable to playing in dirty sunshine.

But when last week's rain cleared, the grey skies gave way to yellowish ones: after its extended break, air pollution was back with a vengeance.

This is very often the pattern. One explanation that I've heard is that the factories to the south of the city, in the Shanghai municipality itself and in Zhejiang province beyond, take advantage of the downpour to burn as much waste as they can. While the rain persists, the resultant miasma is driven into the ground. But when it stops, new clouds of particles quickly fill the skies.

Spot the difference: two dry summer days in Shanghai

In Shanghai, the level of pollution often becomes an obsession, for locals and expats alike. Many people – especially parents – have at least one app on their iPhones that monitors the level of particles in the air. They often have more than one: the official record and one based on the data provided by the US consulate. These seldom match. Both appear to be genuine, though (on rare occasions, the official version gives a worse picture than the US one). It's just that the official one seems to be drawn from advantageously placed monitors (in or around the expansive greenery of Century Park, for example) whereas the US consulate is located in the heart of the downtown Puxi smog.

The difference between the two sides of the Huangpu River is often immediately obvious. From our offices on the Pudong side, facing the

Bund, the river frequently provides a visible demarcation of air quality, with blue(ish) skies to the east and yellow-grey haze obscuring the opposite bank. At other times, there's no distinction, as the whole city is swathed in smog.

When I first visited Shanghai, I thought that the clear blue skies and discreet white clouds of the postcards were the product of airbrushing as much as of photography. But in fact there are days when the sky is gloriously clear, and sometimes – as last August – whole weeks. During the 2010 Expo, there was, friends tell me, a remarkably sustained period of blue skies; factories were shut down or kept under strict controls to ensure that visitors saw Shanghai at its best. When I lived in Beijing in the early 2000s, there was a similar improvement as the city geared up for the Olympic bid. That, alas, did not last.

Beijing's air quality is notorious. When I lived there, I was in the outskirts, in Haidian district; when I ventured downtown, I recall the sky vanishing beneath a sallow haze as one approached the centre. These days, when I visit the city, I stay further out still, in the satellite town of Changping, at the furthest extent of the subway network, close to the Ming tombs. Alas, the smog has ventured further out too. Typically, when I get on the subway train at Changping, the sky is blue. But as the train – which runs overground for the first few stops – makes its way into the city, blue soon gives way to yellowish-grey. The line passes through my old Haidian stomping ground, which today shares the hazy air of the city centre.

The capital certainly faces more difficult geographical – and perhaps cultural – challenges when it seeks to improve its air quality. There are the dust storms that sweep in from the Gobi Desert in spring, and which can turn the sky a hideous ochre shade. And unlike Shanghai, with its proximity to the coast and sea breezes, Beijing is flanked by mountains to its north and west. These provide welcome relief from the urban smog for those seeking to escape from the city, but also serve to trap the dirty air blown in from Tianjin municipality and Shandong province to the south.

Taking the train from Shanghai to Beijing suggests that there's no shortage of foul air waiting to be blown north to the capital. The high-speed train is an impressive beast; it has cut the distance between China's two greatest metropolises from a 17-hour overnight trip to a mere four and a half hours – like a train from London to Edinburgh, except covering two and half times the distance in the same time. And the views from the window are often equally impressive, especially when you pass through the mountains of Shandong. But the views can be depressing too. I've made the trip a number of times and have yet to see anything other than a grey haze hanging over those mountains.

Where culture may be playing a part in exacerbating Beijing's air problem is in the city's undying love affair with the motor car. Traffic fumes account for a substantial proportion of the pollution. Southerners – and perhaps especially Shanghainese – will tell you that Beijingers are particularly "face-conscious". In the seat of government, status, rather than wealth, is the holy grail for many. And nothing speaks of status so much as driving (or being driven in) your own car. It's anecdotal, but I know of many well-off Shanghainese who could afford to take taxis everywhere but instead take the metro. In Beijing, I know car-owners who will always drive, even though it's usually significantly slower than taking the tube. There are road-rationing measures, but they're clearly far from sufficient. They're also deeply unpopular.

Nor is air pollution confined to only the largest Chinese cities. Lanzhou, the capital of Gansu province, is one of the worst offenders. Meanwhile, a Hong Kong native living in Shanghai complains to me of the smog blowing across from Guangdong when he goes home for a visit. And a friend from Yunnan counsels me against visiting Kunming, the provincial capital. This "garden city" is now choked with dust and shrouded in traffic fumes, because of the extensive building work that is underway. One problem is that Chinese construction, while enviably quick first time around, often needs to be revisited frequently. So new roads may close soon after opening, and then at intervals thereafter, as faults are remedied and repairs are made. And the ambitions of property developers often leads to huge building projects that one might think were better completed bit by bit.

Obviously, China's air pollution is a major concern for its population. The facemasks that you see on the street and on sale in convenience stores tell you that, as does the widespread awareness of particle levels. But many people are surprisingly stoical about it. "This is the price we pay for higher living standards", one Shanghai native told me. "And most of us think it's a price worth paying." He may have a point: despite all the murk in their air, the Shanghainese live longer, on average, than Americans.

Some people end up paying a heavier price than others, though. Regardless of the season, there are always people coughing on the Shanghai metro. But it's not the big particles – the ones you cough up – that matter, but the smaller ones that can insinuate their way into your cardiovascular system. Though the mortality rate for serious respiratory diseases fell between 1990 and 2000, it had risen back above its 1990 level by 2009, according to the Chinese Ministry of Health's own figures.

There are signs of progress amid the (figurative and literal) gloom. There is certainly greater transparency, with the authorities now publishing

PM2.5 readings themselves, rather than the less useful (and less alarming) PM10 data. And with all the iPhone apps and internet data available, there is certainly greater public awareness, as manifested in heated discussion in China's blogosphere. But until real improvements materialise, days of rain will always be welcome in Shanghai.

A Letter From China
19 May 2013
Justin Crozier

Chapter 28

The changing face of the Chinese countryside

Most people will be aware of the huge changes that have taken place in China's cities over the past 20 years; even James Bond has used the futuristic towers of Shanghai as a backdrop for his brand of mayhem (though in the Chinese version he doesn't shoot the Chinese guard). Less well known, perhaps, are the changes taking place in China's countryside. This is not surprising: foreigners' visits tend to be confined to the big cities, and even local commentators can be rather urban-centric. However, it is important given the scale involved, a scale that is evident from the window of any Chinese high-speed train, as hour after hour of well-populated rural landscape flashes by.

But I am not going to write about macro trends. I am going to write about one small village called Mulangou. The name can be translated as "Peony Gully", but also summons up the ghost of the famous woman warrior hero Mulan. I first visited Mulangou in 2004. As a personal investment, I rebuilt a farm there in 2005 and have been back regularly ever since. Even using Shandong's fine and lightly trafficked motorway system, Mulangou is a full hour's drive from Yantai, a minor port and the local administrative centre. When I first saw Mulangou it had only a mud road. After a heavy rain the tricky slope up from the neighbouring village became impassable to vehicles. Neither were there any street lamps; when the sun went down it was very dark – nice for star gazing, but little else. Nearly everyone was (and still is) called either Huang or

Gong; I made the classic error of befriending the village head Huang and thus immediately alienating the other half of the village. The population seemed to be made up of the very old (or prematurely aged by working in the fields) and the very young. Men's clothes were the standard blue cotton or khaki, and transport was the walking tractor, ancient bike or muddy motorbike. A car meant that a party official was visiting.

Progress was initially gradual – a distant reflection of the Hu/Wen administration's efforts to improve the lot of the farmers by boosting food prices and improving social security. In 2005 village head Huang suffered a nasty motorbike accident. Like many accidents it happened in the afternoon after a liquid lunch (the Shandong farmers like their baijiu) and without the beneficial intermediation of a helmet. The burden of his hospital treatment fell almost entirely on his family (a daughter who worked in the city). Today Mr. Huang would have received some help from the national rural health-insurance scheme, but that was not in place in 2005. The main road was paved by 2006 (and lined with trees).

I contributed some funds to buy a few street lights and was then sent the bill for the electricity. The makes of motorbike were upgraded. Some farmers bought proper tractors. The quality and variety of younger people's clothing improved. But not all progress is positive. Litter became a terrible problem. Previously, farmers' garbage was largely organic, but now they were shopping at supermarkets. With no rubbish collection, discarded plastic bags and packaging blew across the fields and snagged on the apple trees.

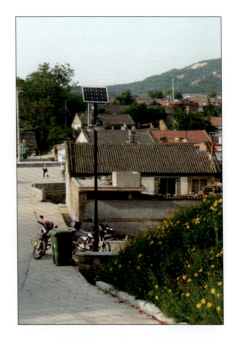

We cut forward to 2013 and to some photographs taken in Mulangou last week. The photo above may look dull at first glance but look again. Solar-powered street lighting! (China has a surplus of solar cells to make use of). And a garbage bin – the local township has now started collecting the rubbish. You will also note that a number of side roads have now been paved.

The number of cars in the village has increased many-fold, especially at the weekend. A car is no longer a sign of a visiting official (though this is still a good bet if it is a black Audi) but of owner-drivers from Yantai or Penglai who are making a family outing to the countryside. A number of the more enterprising farmers now offer genuine countryside lunches, where the visitors can eat very well for Rmb50. A little garden has been laid out in the village centre with, bizarrely, a full set of gymnastic equipment with instructions in English. None of it is ever in use when I pass.

The village is now a veritable hive of construction activity. A new government-sponsored irrigation system has been installed. The hills are dotted with windmills (it is unclear whether any are connected to the grid). A new village hall is being constructed to replace the old one, on which faded red characters exhorting the farmers only to have one child can still be made out. This is an object of pride for the new village head (the only political position in China for which candidates are chosen by popular election). More esoterically, the local businessmen have sponsored the rebuilding of a Taoist temple, knocked down at the time of the Liberation. The philosopher so honoured, one Qiu Chuji, who lived here in the 13th century and advised Genghis Khan, has his birthday in January. When I first arrived this was celebrated by a hundred or so villagers, a bonfire and some fireworks. Now it is a two-day festival, with opera performances and Mulangou's only traffic jam. The local party officials regard the temple as nothing more than a tourist attraction, but I think something more interesting is happening here. I cannot claim that there have been any major advances in agricultural technology or mechanization – the close-planted apple and peach trees do not lend themselves to this. But there seems to be a revival of pride. Although the process of urbanization will continue, and perhaps even accelerate if the new administration brings in hukou reform, the countryside may no longer be just a place from which to escape.

A Letter From China
14 June 2013
Chris Ruffle

Chapter 29

Bread with Chinese characteristics

When I first arrived in Taiwan in 1978, the quality and variety of food was a revelation, certainly in comparison with what was available in the north of England in the 1970s. One of the few disappointments was the scarcity and poor quality of bread. The cardboard-like slabs of pre-sliced bread were only edible toasted with lots of jam, and the biscuits unappetising crumbly affairs, made up of a dry, flaky pastry which could be swallowed only if accompanied by a bowl of tea. There was also the standard birthday cake with pink and turquoise icing, which

Speaks for itself: a Shanghai branch of Bread Talk

could be safely abandoned on the paper plate after the excitement of candle-blowing was concluded. Turnover on the bakery counters was clearly low, and one suspected that the biscuits languishing in their glass displays had been there for a while.

This should not have come as a surprise, perhaps, as baked bread has never been an important part of Chinese cuisine (although steamed bread is still a staple in some poorer parts of the wheat-producing north). Sourcing butter, milk and the right kind of flour was clearly an insuperable problem, and I set aside my occasional craving for a biscuit.

Jump forward to 2013, and bakeries are one of the fastest-growing retail sectors in China. No mall is complete without one or more. There is usually an element of onsite baking, so that the seductive smells can be vented at passers-by. They have names such as Bread Talk, 85° Cafe, Christine (pretending to be French – it's not) or Ichido (it's not Japanese either). The format is similar and self-service: with a pair of large tongs, one selects the desired buns from covered shelves, places them on a tray and goes to the counter for payment and wrapping.

The products themselves have undergone a Chinese transformation. Buns are

The good, the mad and the flaky

163

now topped with rou song (dried pork shavings), dotted with red beans or scattered with a mixed salad of bacon, cheese and sweet corn. Such items have become a staple of the urban, white-collar diet, consumed for breakfast, lunch or a snack, often eaten street-side from their transparent plastic bags. Sandwiches, in contrast, remain unpopular, probably because of the Chinese preference for cooked foods and justified fear of eating cold meats and salads of unknown provenance. Birthday cakes, while still highly coloured, have become more tempting. As for the old flaky pastry, that is now mostly brought back as souvenirs from trips and given to other people to try to digest.

The catalyst for this "Letter from China", which is actually written from the increasingly Chinese city of San Francisco, was your correspondent's discovery, in a Daly City shopping mall, of a modern Chinese bakery. The US is now consuming buns sprinkled with pork shavings, and the story has come full circle. What other one-time Western specialities will soon be served back to Western consumers with Chinese characteristics? Get ready to order your coffee served with sea salt and tapioca balls ...

A Letter From China
25 July 2013
Chris Ruffle

Chapter 30

Emerging markets? No such thing

There is no such thing as "emerging markets". Even when the term was first coined in the 1980s, the concept was little more than an administrative convenience, a slightly patronising shorthand for all those smaller, exotic economies too complicated and volatile to be worth detailed study. Now, however, the terminology is positively misleading. A vast industry built up around the term acts as a drag on attempts to update or redefine the concept. The creation and demise of such acronyms as BRICS, MIKT, Next Eleven and CIVETS are, perhaps, a reflection of how ill "EM" now fits reality. What has China in common with Venezuela? Why should Taiwan and Russia be classified together? And when do we know when we have arrived? In the past 30 years of striving, which market has ever actually "emerged"?

As we look forward to the likelihood of a lower-growth world, it seems that some other groupings might be more helpful than the outdated "emerging markets v. developed markets". "Resource producers v. consumers" is an obvious fault-line running through the heart of the "emerging market" concept. Or a division based on a nation's balance sheet? This could be in monetary terms: "highly leveraged v. unleveraged", or "capital exporters v. capital importers". Or it could refer to the quality of countries' workforces: "old v. young", "better educated v. less well educated".

In a world in which capital can flow with high velocity, constrained only by lack of knowledge, perhaps we ought to abandon the old concept of the nation state as a sensible boundary for investment strategies entirely, moving instead to "emerging industries" or "emerging companies". Look at the top 10 holdings in your emerging-market manager's portfolio; wouldn't an "emerging companies" portfolio be more interesting?

Top 10 stocks in the MSCI Emerging Markets Index	%
Samsung Electronics	3.9
Taiwan Semiconductor Manufacturing	2.4
China Mobile	1.9
China Construction Bank	1.5
Industrial and Commercial Bank of China	1.4
TenCent Holdings	1.4
Gazprom	1.4
America Movil	1.1
CNOOC Ltd	1.0
Hyundai Motor	1.0

(Source: MSCI, as at 31 August 2013)

Of the six Greater Chinese companies featured in this list, we hold none in our specialist China funds at present. We tend not to hold state-owned enterprises, which have a different agenda from minority investors. That rules out four of the six stocks. The other two – TSMC and TenCent – are well-managed companies, which we have owned in the past, but which we now exclude on grounds of valuation.

Emerging markets? No such thing

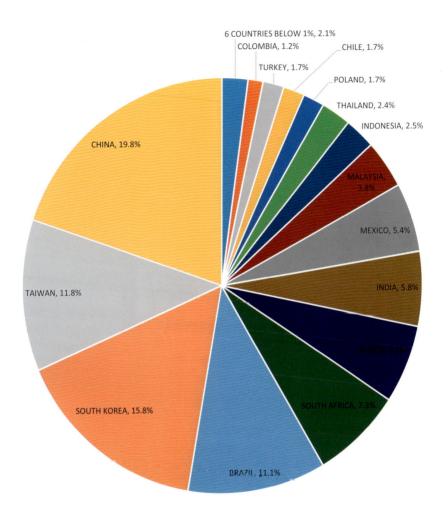

6 COUNTRIES BELOW 1%, 2.1%

COLOMBIA, 1.2%

CHILE, 1.7%

TURKEY, 1.7%

POLAND, 1.7%

THAILAND, 2.4%

INDONESIA, 2.5%

MALAYSIA, 3.8%

CHINA, 19.8%

MEXICO, 5.4%

INDIA, 5.8%

TAIWAN, 11.8%

RUSSIA, 6.1%

SOUTH AFRICA, 7.3%

SOUTH KOREA, 15.8%

BRAZIL, 11.1%

Composition of the MSCI Emerging Market Index by country
(Source: MSCI, as at 31 August 2013)

Greater China now accounts for nearly one-third of "emerging markets", and this is before the imminent entry into the index of China's largest market, the A-share market. Given this, and if you cannot bring yourself to abandon national boundaries, might it not be wise to hire a specialist China-based manager, who can take a bottom-up approach to find the best entrepreneurial companies in China? The list below shows the 10 largest equity holdings in our Greater China strategy:

Stock	%
Clevo	4.1
Yuanta Financial	3.6
Chailease	3.0
China Life Insurance	2.8
Fubon Financial	2.7
Wuxi PharmaTech	2.6
China Lesso Group	2.6
New Oriental Education & Technology Group	2.6
Pactera Technology International	2.4
Xiao Nan Guo Restaurants	2.1

(As of 31 August 2013)

A Letter From China
17 september 2013
Chris Ruffle

Chapter 31

The Fujian Discount

It was still hot in Xiamen when I visited last week. A recent typhoon had swept the city clear of pollution, so the sun's glare was particularly pitiless, and I had to screw up my eyes to see the way ahead. I have suffered from similarly impaired vision over the years with regard to my Fujian investments, the performance of which has been distinctly mixed. We now have only one long-term investment in the province, an autoglass-maker called Fuyao, which is strange when one considers the size of the province (official population 37 million) and its wealth (the China Daily reported its January–August GDP as US$203 billion, +11.2% year on year). I am not alone, however. It is one of the strange truths of the Chinese market that companies in Fujian tend to trade at a discount to similar stocks in other provinces.

"The Fujian Discount" would be an interesting topic for a diligent student embarking on a PhD. Until such a thesis is completed, I can only speculate as to the causes of this phenomenon. First, not to beat about the bush, there is a long history of fraud here. The list of stocks suspended from the Hang Seng is heavily populated with Fujian-based companies, and they account for almost all of the Chinese companies listed in Germany (yes, there are 23 of them). Fujian is far from Beijing and, for much of its history, was cut off by mountains from the interior. There is a long and complicated coastline ideal for smuggling, both in and out (for those interested in more detail on this, I recommend

Oliver August's Inside the Red Mansion about the lurid career of Lai Chanxing). Companies tend to be family-based and concentrated in light industry (garments, shoes, furniture and food) or agriculture. For some reason, about 80% of China's private hospitals are owned by men from the Fujian city of Putian. The province is also close to Taiwan, both physically (you can see Taiwan's Kinmen Island from Xiamen) and culturally (they share the same Minnan dialect).

Chinese culture: new residential blocks going up in Fuzhou

But hope springs eternal, so I visited the province to see if any of the stocks were unduly discounted. We drove from Xiamen via Jinjiang, Putian and Anxi to Fuzhou. My first impression was of the excellence of the motorway system, which enabled such an ambitious schedule. My second was of the sheer scale of the new residential property construction I saw – vast arrays of half-finished or unoccupied apartment blocks. This was most evident in Jinjiang, which is making a big effort, having seen some of its biggest companies, such as sportswear retailer Anta, relocate to Xiamen. But it could also be seen in rural areas, where everywhere farmers were adding extensions on top of their houses; one agricultural company joked that it was difficult to find labour as it was all off mixing cement.

I do not belong to the school of thought, popular in the US, that this will result in some leveraged collapse – most of the property is sold for cash. But it is a sad misallocation of resources and savings to have all this dark property when so many people cannot find affordable housing. I also worry that the poor quality of much of this construction will prove the Chinese perception of property as a gold-bar-like store of value to be false. The case for introducing a nationwide recurring property tax is a strong one. This would both help address chronic local-government funding issues, reducing their dependence on land sales (apparently 45% of the budget in Xiamen), and introduce a cost of carry so that holders of multiple units would be incentivised to rent or sell. The largest property developer in Xiamen discounted my arguments, assuring me that the huge infrastructure investments made by Xiamen were now starting to pay dividends and industrial growth would compensate for any decline in land sale income.

The companies I visited represented a cross-section of the provincial economy. Fujian is famous for its Oolong tea, particularly Tieguanyin. The two tea companies I met (one of which had until recently been a textile company) both complained about how the crackdown on conspicuous consumption by Xi Jinping, a former governor of Fujian, was hurting their high-end tea business. Companies are no longer giving officials gifts of the most fragrant spring-picked Tieguanyin or aged Pu'er. They are now pushing mid- to low-end teas, while hoping that the crackdown will ease by next Chinese New Year. Visiting the tea factory in Anxi, in the midst of beautiful, verdant mountain scenery, I saw numerous brown road signs, showing the way to beauty spots: an indication of the growth of domestic car-based tourism.

Agricultural companies have been hurt by labour-cost inflation. One company we met, Le Gaga, has reacted by concentrating on greenhouse production so as to be able to sell vegetables in the winter season when prices are high. It is now introducing soilless production with drip-feed irrigation, to cut fertiliser and labour input and meet increasingly stringent environmental protection requirements. The inability to source rural land at a reasonable price was a major complaint. Another less fortunate company we met, Asian Bamboo, holds 54,000 hectares of mountainous bamboo plantations, rented for up to 20 years, which it can no longer operate profitably and cannot automate. Le Gaga is one of those "orphan" stocks listed in the wrong market (in this case the US) and now in the process of privatisation. Asian Bamboo remains happy with its listing in Germany.

Chairlady Chiu and CEO Ma of Le Gaga illustrate the new soilless way of growing peppers

The young CEO of a wrapping-tissue company claimed that business was steady as exporters sought a cheap way to upgrade products. He felt, however, that based on his own experience and the unwillingness of his peers to make new investments, official GDP growth numbers are overstated. This company counters cost-inflation issues through its de-inking process, which allows it to source 60% of its pulp from waste paper. Two of its new projects reflect the changing Chinese lifestyle – it is working to supply McDonald's with wrapping paper for its hamburgers, which is now imported from Japan, and has also started to make backing paper for wallpaper.

Moving further downstream, I visited a candy manufacturer where business is growing steadily. This company produces a vast range of jellies, chocolates and other sweets; the very air around the factory smells of sugar. This is one of the few visits when it would have been useful to have my younger daughter along, as the CEO enthusiastically urged us to sample his wares. The company spends 8–10% of revenues on advertising and makes extensive use of character merchandising (Angry Birds seems par-

With Yongyou CEO Ke and one day's supply of pulp

ticularly popular). Although based in Fujian, the company has a nation-wide production network with factories in Tianjin, Sichuan, Anhui and, shortly, Hubei. It looks to follow in the path of rivals Want Want and Tingyi by expanding from its speciality into wider consumer products. Consequently, it has recently launched a range of fruit-flavoured milkd drinks with the help of rising actress Yang Mi.

Chairman Zheng's new banana milk comes in two types of packaging

Electronics plays a substantial role in the Fujian economy, often Taiwan-invested. I visited only one technology firm on this trip, however, a slightly creepy company called Meiya Pico, which specialises in "digital forensic investigations". In some ways the company is admirable, being spun out of Xiamen University and spending heavily on R&D (15% of sales). But its main customer is the Public Security Bureau and its main role is helping this organisation to police the web and extract information from mobile phones. It claims to be an "Eric Snowden beneficiary", now that the government has realised that it should not buy foreign security equipment or software. The downside, as with all companies dependent on government sales, is payment. The CFO assured me that his invoices are usually paid within one year, and at the very latest, within three.

I enjoyed my road trip to Fujian, even though it has not, as yet, resulted in any new buys. Thinking back to my first visit to Fujian in the 1980s, not only has there been a revolution in the ease of travel, but also a huge improvement in places to stay. Jinjiang offered me a Marco Polo Hotel and Putian a Doubletree Hilton. The service was good and, being rather quiet at present, they were able to offer me a discount. A Fujian discount.

A Letter From China
29 september 2013
Chris Ruffle

Chapter 32

Games without frontiers

An unexpected burst of nostalgia overcame me as I walked homewards through the warren that is the Shanghai Science & Technology Museum metro station. The long corridor leading to my exit was newly emblazoned with lurid scenes of battle between men, monsters and magicians. But rather than any of the gods and demons drawn from Chinese mythology that crop up in domestic computer games and cartoons, these fantastical forms were distinctly Occidental in form. The British wargaming company Games Workshop was opening a new store.

Marching east: A sign advertising the new Games Workshop store in Shanghai

It took me back to the 1980s Britain of my childhood: to Saturday afternoons filled with endless manoeuvring of little lead hobgoblins and half-orcs across commandeered kitchen tables. Back then, Games Workshop was just emerging as the leading British producer of fantasy games. I knew that it had since become an international company, but I had no idea that it was operating in China.

It was a couple of days to the opening of the new store, but I discovered that there was already one up and running in Xintiandi, an area of downtown Shanghai where traditional shikumen houses have been expensively recreated to function as homes, restaurants and boutiques. With its displays of tiny legions of orcs and elves, it looked incongruous amid all the pricey boutiques in the upmarket Xintiandi Style shopping mall.

Yet here it was – and here it had been for two years. Amid the miniature scenery and serried ranks of dwarfs and space marines, I spoke to Games Workshop employee Liang, who, in fluent English, gave me a run-down on the gaming scene in Shanghai. He reckoned that the Xintiandi shop has between 100 and 150 regular customers. That doesn't sound a lot, but with a box of elves or goblins going for 600 or 700 kuai (£60–70) and a fair few of those needed to fight the typical battle, those customers are relatively high rolling.

I was surprised to learn that nearly all are adults; I had envisaged the typical customers as "little emperors" with indulgent parents. But Liang told me that they were generally in their twenties and thirties, and in well-paid jobs. Most, he said, came to tabletop wargaming through computer games like World of Warcraft, which owes more than a little to Games Workshop's tabletop game Warhammer.

In particular, said Liang, the computer hit Dawn of War drove customers to the science-fiction version, by dint of being set in Games Workshop's sci-fi universe. I spoke to some customers in the shop, who confirmed that this had been the "gateway drug" for them.

Computer games, of course, are widely pirated in China, as are so many other things, from DVDs to dictionaries. Games Workshop's figurines (now largely plastic rather than the lead-based alloy of my childhood) look highly vulnerable to piracy. A quick look at Taobao, China's ebay, revealed a legion of Warhammer soldiers available from a seller in Shenyang. Whether or not these are pirate copies is unclear, but here one's suspicions naturally incline to their being fakes. So how does the company tackle the pirate threat?

One measure is not manufacturing its miniatures in China. The firm uses Chinese factories to make its paints and brushes, but confines production of the higher-end stuff to the UK and the US. Thus it avoids one of the most common forms of Chinese piracy, whereby a genuine factory simply churns out a few extra products each day, which are then profitably spirited to the myriad "fake markets" in the city centres.

But Liang told me that the firm has another weapon with which to combat the knock-offs: community. The Shanghai store hosts regular in-house games and tournaments, in which only legitimate models can be used. This attitude has rubbed off, according to Liang, with players refusing to play with those who field pirated models even in the privacy of their own homes. One suspects that there's a kind of snobbery or status-consciousness involved here: tabletop wargaming is an expensive hobby, and those with the wealth to indulge in it doubtless want to preserve that exclusive cachet.

Elf service: Liang in the Xintiandi store

Now, the idea of toy soldiers enjoying any kind of cachet might strike Western readers as odd. Socially acceptable as the computerised variants may have become, tabletop wargaming is still seen as the domain of the nerd. In China, however, there is no "nerd stigma". Indeed, it's arguable that the very concept of "nerd" doesn't exist. A fascinating discussion on the linguistics blog Language Log considers this proposition in some depth.

Given that, I suspect Games Workshop are onto something in China. A few months ago, I asked my colleagues how they would define "middle class" in China. One of the answers was "having the time and money to pursue hobbies". Tabletop wargaming might be a somewhat shamefaced pastime in the West, but in China it, like any other activity demanding leisure time and expense, speaks of wealth and status.

There's another social dimension too. In the West, many typically male hobbies are often seen as things to be tolerated at best by wives or girlfriends. They lack the healthy and athletic associations of sport, and are seen instead as rather anoraky obsessions. This may well be unfair, but an advertised fondness for wargames or toy soldiers would be unlikely to improve one's chances in online dating. In China's ferociously competitive marriage market, though, "nerdy" pursuits are no handicap and may even improve the odds.

Dicey situations: the Chinese rules of Warhammer

For one thing, the male leisure pursuits that are viewed positively in the West – principally sport – are often seen as an oafish waste of time in China. At school, participation in sport is discouraged by ambitious Chinese parents, who fear that it will eat into study time. For another, "socialising" can also be suspect in China. While going out and having a drink with friends or colleagues is regarded as wholesome in Western countries, it's something that Chinese spouses (and in-laws) tend to frown on. In a country where nightlife frequently shades into something murkier, if you're playing with toy soldiers, you're not pursuing the shadier pastimes of the affluent Chinese man: wining, dining and singing karaoke, perhaps with professional "hostesses". In that context, it's easy to see why a harmless, if eccentric, pastime might be preferred in a husband or boyfriend.

And who knows? Perhaps fantasy wargaming won't turn out to be an almost exclusively male pastime in China. The most surprising aspect of my visit to the Xintiandi Games Workshop was when Liang told me that the winner of the store's last tournament was female.

A Letter From China
1 October 2013
Justin Crozier

Chapter 33

Corporate risk in China

China is a risky place. All international investors are well aware of this. If you are not, there is an army of short-sellers only too keen to reveal to you the horrors of investing in China – all in the public interest, of course. Your correspondent has encountered a number of these risks in his 23 years of company visiting here. This letter is an attempt to delineate such risks and suggest some ways of mitigating them.

Risks can be mitigated through vigilance and rigour ...

China today is a fertile ground for corporate risk. The one-party system, combined with the lack of a free press or independent judiciary, results in endemic corruption. A state-owned banking system lending chiefly to the state-owned sector forces many in the private sector, now 70% of the economy, to look to "shadow finance". Lack of currency convertibility on the capital account, combined with a shallow domestic market for equities and bonds, particularly in the early years, has led to Chinese stocks now being listed over several different exchanges, with varying degrees of liquidity. The ever-changing regulatory framework also exacerbates a natural tendency to focus on short-term profit.

Given this murky operating environment, we find the key determinant in assessing the type and extent of corporate risk is whether a company is state-owned or privately owned. For state-owned enterprises (SOEs) the key problem is the lack of a sense of ownership among employees; it is not their company. The problem therefore tends to be value extraction, either through an inflation of costs or establishing management-owned entities – typically a supplier or a sales company – that take a tithe from the SOE. Often we find SOEs seeking scale for its own sake – the expansion in employee numbers and SGA (selling, general and administrative) costs at some of the larger SOEs has been heroic. Alternatively, SOEs end up working towards political goals, with little thought to the rate of return in a new officially sanctioned project. Internal risk controls can be weak, which can prove particularly damaging in the finance sector.

At privately owned enterprises (POEs), interests should be better aligned with those of investors. Here the key is to clarify who the real owners are, where their money came from and what other assets are owned but not injected into the listed company. Typical problems at a POE are the inflation of sales and profits to boost the initial public offering or the faking of contracts or invoices under pressure from lenders or outside parties. The need for smaller private borrowers to rely on "unconventional" financing can also lead to high costs. Overall, our experience has been that there is more fraud at state-owned companies than at privately owned companies. The problem is that the Bank of China will remain the Bank of China, however many times it is robbed by its own employees. When private company owners are found to have put a hand in the till there is rarely any way back.

Is the location of listing of Chinese companies relevant when considering the likelihood of fraud? There certainly seems to be a correlation between distance from China and corporate risk, with Nasdaq, Singapore and AIM all having an above-average share of unreliable corporates. The "SPAC" (special-purpose acquisition company) or "blank cheque" system of fund-raising in the US has proved particularly disastrous. Of the main markets, your correspondent has been sandbagged more often in "laissez-faire" Hong Kong than in either Taiwan or the A-share market,

Watch out for employees with their hands in the till ...

where fund-raising is centrally controlled by the SFC and CSRC, respectively. The superior liquidity of the Taiwanese and A-share markets also aids escape, when compared with the variable liquidity available in Hong Kong and that market's penchant for suspending listings for prolonged periods. The custom of Hong Kong companies granting themselves a general mandate to issue up to 30% new shares at every AGM has been a particular source of grief, and I urge all readers to vote against such motions.

For those readers who are still with me after this litany of horror, I would like to suggest some methods I have found useful in mitigating the "China risk":

- Always physically visit the target companies. In a place as large as China, this can be tedious, especially when stocks are moving, but it is better to be safe than sorry. Numbers lie, and managements can be economical with the truth, but I have found factories, shops or building sites to provide the best indication there is of a company's prospects.

- Triangulate results by talking with the company's rivals, suppliers or customers. The rival is always the most willing to dish the dirt on his competitor.

- Are margins in line with those of the company's peers? If not, why not?

- Company accounts in China are on an improving trend, but special attention still needs to be paid to receivables, intra-group transactions and any mismatches in the currency or duration of debt.

- If a company ticks all the boxes, don't go all in – gradually build up a position as confidence grows in management's ability to deliver on promises.

Once invested, a manager should diarise regular updates with the company. Aside from changes in fundamentals or valuation, there are a number of developments that we have found to be red flags, which, while individually not necessarily causing a sale, should prompt close questioning of management:

- Insider selling

- Change of auditor (especially to a local firm) or CFO

- Regular fund-raisings

- Ill-considered diversification

- Unjustifiable acquisition or disposal of assets (especially if from or to a related party)

This letter will now veer into more subjective territory in recommending types of Chinese companies to avoid. This is not scientific, but the result of prejudices built up over a number of years, so I ask for the reader's indulgence.

- Don't invest in a profitable company that does not pay a dividend. In China, dividends have a value greater than the apparent yield; I have never been defrauded by a company paying me a decent dividend.

- Don't invest in any company where the ultimate owner is related to the army or security apparatus. You are not going to win.

- Don't invest in any company which operates in a politically sensitive area (e.g. media) or boasts of its strong political guanxi. Politicians come and go.

- Don't invest in property developers (the heart of corruption in China and terribly difficult to value) or agriculture (there's always a new disease or natural disaster just around the corner).

- Don't invest in any company in Fujian. Any experienced Chinese manager will be able to tell you about the "Fujian discount".

- Don't invest in companies where the spokesperson is missing the tip of a finger or is very attractive.

In conclusion, corporate governance risk in China is high, but my sense is that the perception of risk is even higher. This leads to neglected investment opportunities which can be exploited by experienced managers willing to travel hard and keep their eyes open. Just remember to count the number of fingers ...

A Letter From China
5 October 2013
Chris Ruffle

Chapter 34

The China Dream

A new propaganda campaign now covers bill boards and building sites across China, but this one is unlike any I have seen before. The typical Communist propaganda poster is red and features slogans of Animal Farm simplicity ("Serve the People!") or impenetrable opacity ("Strongly uphold the Three Represents!"). There is often a picture of the Great Wall with guardians of the proletariat staring heroically into the middle distance. Not here.

This is the poster which first caught my eye. It features a painting by one of my favourite modern artists, Feng Zikai (1898–1975). A man on a horse views a tree that has been cut down, or at least brutally pruned, but is regrowing. The large characters say "Chinese culture will live on, without pause". The accompanying poem, by Kun Yin, says:

I have been many places

I have seen all sorts of things

But today, halting my horse and looking back

My tears write these two lines:

The roots of the Chinese people are deep

They will come back through difficulties to the light

Along the top it reads:

> Civilization and good manners; Public service advertisement; China spirit; China form; China culture; China achievement

At the bottom it is branded with a red seal stamped "China Dream".

What are we to make of all this? My first interpretation was that harm has been done to the Chinese people/environment (by previous administrations?) but now everything is going to be all right.

There are other Feng Zikai posters that are also attractive but less difficult to interpret. In this one a doctor (looking a little like Karl Marx?) listens to a globe with his stethoscope, and big characters state "The Globe. There is only one." Two men, with arms round each other's shoulder (perhaps drunk?), stagger past the Chinese characters which say "Friendship is more valuable than gold".

There is another series which shares the same branding (white background and the China Dream stamp) but revolves around ceramic models of children. These are rather twee, but I guess have a similar appeal to pictures of kittens. The children are all dressed in old-fashioned clothing, as in the picture below. We are to gather from the poem by Lu Yiqing that this is a poor boy from the mountains, who nevertheless loves his books. The big characters read "Honesty makes for a happy home, poetry and books for a long life".

Other accomplishments such as music, calligraphy and even sports are extolled by cute children wielding zither, paintbrush and ball, respectively. The Confucian virtues of "filial piety" and "goodness" are also extolled. But perhaps the most iconic poster, certainly it seems the most frequent, is one showing a fat little girl in padded jacket, hair tied into a bunch with a red string, squatting and staring wistfully into space. The title says simply "China's dream. My dream". A third series of less interesting posters share the branding, but feature dull folk art and more obvious sentiments.

So why are we now the subject of this strange new poster campaign, perhaps the biggest, and certainly the most varied, since the Cultural Revolution? The tone is frankly nostalgic, casting back to the good old, bad old days, days when the China dream was more than a busy shopping mall and an apartment on the fourth ring road. The concern with ethics, and the restoration of Confucian and even Taoist precepts (apparently Xi comes from a Taoist family), is perhaps a reaction to the steady stream of food and drug safety scandals, in which corner-cutting producers put their fellow citizens' lives at risk. Even the Communist Party now seems to feel the loss of trust in a society in which the Cultural Revolution was followed by breakneck growth and increasing inequality; lacking the right tools in their own Marxist-Leninist-Maoist kit bag, they are reaching back to more traditional ways of viewing the world. It is easy to understand why a fast-ageing society should want to stress the importance of looking after your parents. The environmental damage of two decades of rapid growth must also be obvious to the leaders living in Zhongnanhai in the middle of Beijing's smog.

Xi Jinping has claimed that the China Dream has his own catchphrase, in clear reference to, and opposition with, the American Dream. But whereas in English the phrase "I have a dream" conjures up Martin Luther, a goal to be sought and eventually reached, in Chinese the first person that comes to mind is the Taoist philosopher Zhuangzi, who on waking from his butterfly dream wondered that he might perhaps be a butterfly dreaming that he was a man. In Chinese the concept of a dream is more insubstantial and difficult of attainment. "Ni zuo meng" is as well used as "You must be dreaming". What do Xi and the Communist Party mean by the China Dream? Well, we are about to find out, when the new administration lays out its reform program at the forthcoming Third Plenum in November. Let's hope they are not just blowing bubbles.

A Letter From China
22 October 2013
Chris Ruffle

Chapter 35

Meeting China

There are 68 notebooks on a shelf behind my desk. These record my meetings with Chinese companies since 1995. Earlier ones have been misplaced in various office moves, but there are still several thousand meetings recorded. Despite disparaging comments from my iPad-armed colleagues, I still think much of the value of a company meeting lies in writing it up afterwards, so I continue to use notebooks.

The bulk of meetings are in the visited company's premises. These involve a lot of hard travelling, but I think site visits can tell you a lot about a company. How efficient is it, how labour-intensive, how busy, how many empty desks, how much inventory? This is more useful, I find, than managements coming into my office. They usually do this only when they are looking for money or votes (even in the case of the mischievously named "non-deal roadshows").

On the Tibetan plateau, notebook in hand ...

The other major category is companies met at broker conferences. While more relaxed delegates sit downstairs in the main auditorium listening to strategists and economists expatiate about the macroeconomy and scroll through their iPads, there is a whole hidden world upstairs; analysts dash in and out of hotel rooms (with beds removed) in a form of corporate speed-dating. The benefit is that you can see a lot of companies in a short space of time; out on the mean streets of Beijing or Taipei, four meetings in a day is a pretty good achievement. In a broker conference, it is quite possible to see seven or eight. If you are a sufficiently important client for the broker, or the company is sufficiently unpopular, you can enjoy one-on-one meetings. If not, you are lumped into a "group meeting". These tend to be unsatisfactory, as the group has different levels of knowledge of the company, as well as varying levels of language skill ("mixed-ability classes", as they called them in secondary school). Questions need to be asked in a certain order, but with a group there is an inevitable jumping back and forth. The sole benefit is to hear what other analysts think is important about a company.

In terms of the company's representation, the normal rule is that state-owned enterprises will field more people than a private company. With SOEs you will only get to see the top leadership on the IPO roadshow or at an AGM. Generally, the seniority of the representative is in inverse relation to company size. In the early days, A-share companies lagged in terms of corporate disclosure: "Who are you and why are you asking these questions?" But with the growing institutionalization of the A-share market, the situation has improved, and a well-informed board secretary usually takes investor meetings. My heart sinks when I am introduced to an "IR manager" who joined the company last month.

When visiting a company, after it has been established whom your appointment is with, you are shown into an empty meeting room. The old

Some company representatives wear uniform ...

Mao-style meeting room, where you sat side by side in armchairs, is now dying out. More often the venue is a boardroom with an overly large polished table. When alone, sitting in the centre seems unnaturally formal, so I usually sit towards one end (if you want to unsettle the company rep, sit at the end in the chairman's seat). You will be brought tea or warm water (it's good for you – really). If you are offered "tea or coffee", don't fall into the trap of choosing coffee – this rarely ends well. Look around. In addition to dull corporate art, there may be some calligraphy, some "good supplier" certificates or photographs of important communist politicians visiting the company ("So that's what the owner looks like!"). Most useful is when there is a display of the company's products, so you can gain a rough idea of what the widget is before the discussion starts. In some consumer-product companies you might be asked to sample the company's wares. For politeness's sake, this cannot be avoided, and is usually relatively painless. The most difficult challenge I faced in this regard was being asked to sample a company's sausages having just been shown round its factory (I agree with Bismarck's comment that with laws as with sausages, it is better not to see them being made.)

One of the most dangerous items you can find in a meeting room is the already-prepared screen and projector. "Death by Corporate Video" beckons (is it the same American who does all these voiceovers?). Such videos, with their high-sounding mission statements and stirring music, are only useful if the analyst has not properly prepared the meeting (shame

... others take a less formal approach

on you!). On the whole, I have found Chinese companies pretty friendly and happy to share what they know. Starting with some easy questions to put them at their ease works well. Establishing the company's origins and ownership structure is important and uncontroversial, as is understanding the experience of the person sitting opposite. In cases where companies are prickly it is usually because they are being criticised for poor performance or corporate-governance failures. Whether the criticisms are justified is for the analyst to find out, but a little sympathy and demonstrating knowledge of the company's business can soothe sensitivities over the course of a meeting.

I always try not to outstay my welcome – one hour is usually sufficient (and I have the representative's name card if I want to follow up later).

It is also important to leave time for a tour around a factory, store or building site, if such is possible. Not only can much be learned about a company's operations this way, but the spokesman is often more forthcoming than in a more formal meeting – which can be both good and bad, depending on what you are told and whether it is actionable afterwards!* Meetings over lunch can also be useful in this regard, though it is difficult to take notes (as the stains on some of my notebooks attest). I have sampled a number of company canteens in this way and can report an improving quality over my years of company visiting in China.

I have not included here any of my more bizarre meeting experiences: the one in an earthquake when my counterparty disappeared beneath his desk; the one in Hohhot where I arrived early to find my host flat out asleep on top of his desk; one in the early days to a Chinese bank, where I came out of the meeting with no more than the bank's address. But I hope that I have given a sense of what it is like to meet China. Now to fill my 69th notebook...

* Note to the investing police: Chinese companies are now well aware of the meaning of "material non-public information". In visits to A-share companies, visiting analysts must often sign a form to say they have got none. As the CSRC has matured as a market regulator we've noticed a significant number of companies now adopting this type of form in furtherance of their quarterly disclosure requirement to list all their visiting analysts with the authorities.

A Letter From China
25 November 2013
Chris Ruffle

Chapter 36

What's in a (Chinese) name?

If names be not correct, language is not in accordance with the truth of things. If language is not in accordance with the truth of things, then affairs cannot be carried on to success.

Analects, Book XIII, Chapter 3

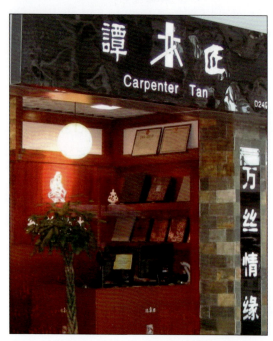

If I were a carpenter ...

What a company is called is, as Confucius would doubtless have agreed, very important. The origins of the names of Chinese companies are more varied than the Western equivalents. There are few companies which bear their founder's surname à la Dell, Templeton or WH Smith. This is not perhaps surprising when over 20% of the population has three surnames (for the record, Wang 7.1%, Li 7.0% and Zhang 6.7%).

That being said, we do have Lee's Pharmaceuticals and Yip's Chemicals, and the chairman of massage-chair-maker OSIM is Mr Sim. The only founder to get his whole name featured is Li Ning, the former gymnast who won nine Olympic golds for China. A personal favourite is Carpenter Tan, which tells us that Mr Tan is good at woodwork. More frequent use is made in China of personal names, which are more varied than Christian names in the West. The electrical-appliance manufacturer and retailer Tsann Kuen (灿坤) was established by Mr Wu Tsann Kuen. The Chinese name of 360Buy (京东), one of China's largest e-commerce companies, is made up of parts of the first names of the founder (刘强东) and his ex-girlfriend (罗小京).

Many of the older or more traditional companies make use of characters from The Book of Changes or other ancient texts. Much-used characters include 德 ("virtue"), 仁 ("humanity"), 信 ("trust"), 义 ("righteousness"), 泰 ("solidity"), 和 ("harmony") and 昌 ("prosperity"). Many Chinese company names are prefixed with the city or province of origin, which is a function of domestic registration procedures, but these are being discarded as businesses become more national. In Chinese, "Anhui" has been dropped from Anhui Conch Cement, which now makes the majority of its cement outside the province. A number of company names are an elision of the place and the product; for example, Shantui (山推, literally "mountain" and "push") makes bulldozers in Shandong, and Shanshui (山水) makes cement in the same province. The medical-device-maker Weigao (威高, gao being "high") is based in Weihai and makes high-tech products. Slightly trickier is the widespread use of the traditional name for provinces; these are the characters you see on car number plates. The shirt-maker Luthai (鲁泰) combines the old name for Shandong with one of the "good" characters listed above. The 3C retail chain Suning is from Nanjing (old name Ning) in Jiangsu.

The table below shows China's provinces with their Chinese characters

省/直辖市	Province	简称	Pinyin
北京市	Beijing	京	Jing
天津市	Tianjin	津	Jin
上海市	Shanghai	沪	Hu
重庆市	Chongqing	渝	Yu
河北省	Hebei	冀	Ji
山西省	Shanxi	晋	Jin
辽宁省	Liaoning	辽	Liao
吉林省	Jiling	吉	Ji
黑龙江省	Heilongjiang	黑	Hei
江苏省	Jiangsu	苏	Su
浙江省	Zhejiang	浙	Zhe
安徽省	Anhui	皖	Wan
福建省	Fujian	闽	Min
江西省	Jiangxi	赣	Gan
山东省	Shandong	鲁	Lu
河南省	Henan	豫	Yu
湖北省	Hubei	鄂	Er
湖南省	Hunan	湘	Xiang
广东省	Guangdong	粤	Yue
海南省	Hainan	琼	Qiong
四川省	Sichuan	川	Chuan
贵州省	Guizhou	黔	Qian
云南省	Yunnan	滇	Dian
陕西省	Shanxi	陕	Shan
甘肃省	Gansu	甘	Gan
青海省	Qinghai	青	Qing
西藏自治区	Xizang (Tibet)	藏	Zang
广西	Guangxi	桂	Gui
内蒙古	Inner Mongolia	蒙	Meng
宁夏	Ningxia	宁	Ning
新疆	Xinjiang	新	Xin

(left/hand column) and traditional names abbreviated to a single character (third column from the left).

Chinese history has left its mark on Chinese company names. The popularity of the character ding (鼎), as in the engineering company CTCI (中鼎) harks back to the ritual bronze tripods of the Zhou dynasty. The popularity of Datang (大唐) is because these companies are laying claim to the greatness of the Tang dynasty. The more recent Communist planned-economy period has, in contrast, left surprisingly little trace on listed companies. We still have First Tractor and First Auto, but Second Auto has now changed its name to Dongfeng (东风, East Wind). After all, who wants to be second, let alone No.5, Special Steel Works (long ago merged into Baoshan Steel)? One of the best hospitals in Beijing, however, is still No.301 Hospital. There are also some more broadly patriotic names – a privately managed convenience store chain in Chengdu is called Hongqi (红旗, "red flag") and there are several Zhongxings (中兴, "China arising") and a Wah Lee (华立, "China upstanding"). More poetically, we have Aurora (震旦, "Eastern dawn"), a fancy name for a firm that makes office furniture.

The internet age has given a new lease of life to the Chinese love of numerology. A recruitment company is called 51 Job because, in Chinese, 51 sounds like "I want". (A Taiwanese recruitment company also uses a number, 104, but this is because that is also the number for Taiwanese directory enquiries.) Similarly, the number for the recently listed 58.com was chosen as it sounds like "I get rich". The liking for numerology also extends to the choice of stock codes; it is not a coincidence that the lottery operator Rexlot has a stock code of 555, or that the traditional-medicine firm Sanjiu ("three nines") has the code 999.

The rise of capitalism in China has led companies to choose a new array of characters reflecting new values: popular characters are 发展 ("development"), 利 ("profit"), 盛 ("prosperous"), 荣 ("glory") and 长 ("growth"). The only listed company I have come across in China to be founded by a Muslim is called Zhongyin Cashmere (中银绒业), the first two characters chosen in gratitude for early help from the Bank of China (中国银行).

Once the Chinese name is established, another consideration is how to transpose it into English. If the name is simply romanised, then the pinyin system is usually used on the mainland and the older Wade Giles system in Taiwan; what is Zhongxing on the mainland is Chung Hsing in Taiwan. An exception is that some companies on the mainland with a claim to an illustrious history romanise their name using Wade Giles – notably Tsingtao Beer (should be Qingdao) and Kweichou Moutai (should be Guizhou Maotai). Sometimes this can be a little unwieldy for an English speaker – anyone for Haoxiangni Jujubes (好想你, literally "I miss you, small red fruit")? When the Cantonese dialect is used this can sound unpleasant; it is good that Luk Fook (六福, "six happiness") is retailing its gold jewellery to an exclusively Chinese audience. Fook Woo (福和, "happy together"), on the other hand, has just changed its name to the more prosaic Integrated Waste Solutions. Sometimes the method decided upon is to use an English word that sounds more or less like the Chinese; the KTV-lounge operator 好乐迪 (haoledi, literally "good music disco") comes out pretty well as Holiday. The Hunan-based construction-machinery company Zoomlion has a certain je ne sais quoi (the Chinese name 中联, Zhonglian, refers to Confucius' Golden Mean). Sincere Navigation sounds as though it is a translation, but is actually a "sounds like" example; the original 新兴, hsin hsing, means "newly arising". It is a good thing they don't sell used cars.

In a large number of cases, Chinese companies have worked backwards and chosen a name that appears to be a translation of a foreign name, on the basis that foreign goods are of higher quality or superior technology. The appliance giant Haier now dwarfs the German equipment-maker Liebherr from which it derived its name. Andre Juice bought its first equipment from a company called An-

Airmate (or Aimeite): the name makes no sense in Chinese

dre. Wumart (物美, "goods beautiful") might have been thinking of another large international retailer. The name "Airmate" makes perfect sense in English for China's leading electric-fan-maker, but it makes absolutely no sense in Chinese. It is difficult to know where the founder of the gloriously named fashion retailer Meters Bonwe derived his inspiration (Hungary, perhaps?). In Taiwan, there are a number of companies named to sound like Japanese companies. Oda Precision (大田) makes golf-club heads and Taiwan Sakura (台湾樱花) makes kitchens, but the only one I have found on the mainland is ramen-noodle chain Ajisen (味千拉面). When I first met the children's wear retailer Les Enphants and hesitantly mentioned that the French don't spell it that way, I was re-assured that the "ph" stood for the company motto, "peace and harmony". So that's all right then.

There are some examples of the regrettable use of initials, so widely employed by Western companies. In the case of CITIC, non-Chinese readers are not missing much (中信, "China Trust"), but for SITC (海丰, "sea fertility") and TCI (大江生医, "great river medical") I think the use of initials is a shame.

I would like to round out this brief note on the art of Chinese company names with a highly speculative and contentious claim. Chinese companies with the character 大 ("big") in their names tend to underperform. Think of Chaoda (超大, "super big", Tatung (see above), Tafu (大福) and First Telecom (大众). My reasoning for this is that the claim is hubristic. I guess the lift-maker Yungtay (永大, "forever big") and broker Yuanta (元大, "big money") have done OK so far but, lacking a willing PhD student, I think my claim still holds. Finally, I would like to end with a Greater China portfolio chosen exclusively on the basis of their bizarre English names. (Note to investment police: we are nearing Christmas and this is a joke. I am not seriously recommending investors to choose investments on their names. Though I have seen some less well-founded systems...)

Jazz Hipster (6247 TT)
Honey Hope Honesty (8043 TT)
Makalot (1477 TT) – they do
Thunder Tiger (8033 TT) – remote-control toys
Le Gaga (GAGA US) – nothing to do with the pop star. A Taiwanese aboriginal life code.
Swellfun (600779 CH) – Diageo has a stake
Sparkle Roll (970 HK) – sells Bentleys and Rollers
Homey Aquatic (600467 CH)
Tell How Science (600590 CH)
Louis XIII (577 HK) – the one before Louis XIV
O My God (3687 TT)

A Letter From China
27 November 2013
Chris Ruffle

Chapter 37

A numbers game

One of the many things that Shanghai residents like to complain about is that they need to pay for the right to have a car. This is called the "number-plate auction" and has been in place since 1994. Its purpose is to control the ownership of private cars in the city.

Although owning a car in Shanghai is not quite as expensive as owning one in Singapore, the Shanghai auction price has risen relentlessly over the past decade. The average number-plate price hit a historical high of around Rmb92,000 in March 2013, up from Rmb14,700 in January 2002.

The author's hard-won number plate

This steep rise is explained by the fall in the average price of passenger cars, thanks to intensive competition, and by rising disposable incomes. Meanwhile, demand continues to outstrip supply. In recent years, the monthly quota for the number-plate auction has usually been around 9,000, while the number of auction participants tends to be around 20,000. Some people try to register their cars outside Shanghai, but there are costs and inconveniences involved, so the majority of hopeful car owners still choose to participate in the auction.

Although it comes in for constant criticism, the plate-auction system is the most practical way of controlling the volume of cars on Shanghai's streets. To register for the bid, which is carried out online between 10 and 11:30 am on the third Saturday of each month, you need to pay Rmb100. You also need to make a Rmb2,000 downpayment, which will be forfeited should you choose not to proceed after successfully bidding.

The bidding itself is divided into two parts, the free bid and the price mark-up. During the free bid, which lasts an hour, you need to bid once for a minimum of Rmb100. But the real trick is to get the half-hour-long mark-up bidding right. Amazingly, you can see the lowest winning price (LWP) in real time throughout the bidding. So you get two chances, but since the LWP keeps moving up, you only get a meaningful shot near the close of bidding. You look at the current LWP, add a maximum of Rmb300 (a measure designed both to keep prices from flying ever higher and to limit your chance of winning), fire in your number and click your mouse frantically to submit your bid online.

Since the process of submitting a bid takes about 20 seconds, the final LWP usually appears at about 11:29:40. If you enter your bid too early, others will easily outbid you. But you can't leave it too late, as you may miss out altogether. Nor can you afford any typing errors. In our first bid, my wife timed everything right, but then entered the wrong digit by mistake (easily done when you've only got 20 seconds to work with). By the time she had corrected it, the auction was over. So we failed miserably. My wife said that her nerves wouldn't stand undergoing the ordeal again.

Better than the stockmarket? The rise in Shanghai number-plate prices over the past decade

So, next month was my turn. After scrutinising the rules of the game, I found out that the first part is not just a waste of time. I could put in a relatively big price that was acceptable to me and hope to win the bid early on. Given the publicly available supply and demand numbers and the price trend, I entered a bid 15% higher than the previous month's average winning price in the first minute and didn't look at my screen again until the bid was over. I won easily, but then discovered with some regret that the actual month-on-month increase hadn't been as large as I had expected. I then realised that the auction authorities publish the lowest winning price and the average winning price, but not the highest, in order to save face for those who, like me, have bid too high.

Given that passenger cars are not a necessity in urban China, I think that this auction system has been successfully refined by Shanghai's technocrats. But after the plate price hit its all-time high of Rmb92,000 in March 2013, the Shanghai government came under huge pressure to reform the system. The authorities finally yielded, introducing a new feature called the warning price (around the average of the previous month) and changing the system so that higher bids are not accepted in the first part of the auction. This serves to cap the winning price, making the price-mark-up bid the crucial part of the auction. As a result, number-plate prices have been declining for the past few months and are now around Rmb75,000. The auction authorities can decide whether or not to activate the warning price. This means that we can expect plate prices to trade in a narrow range from now on.

As the traffic situation continues to worsen in China's major cities, it is unsurprising to see the other local authorities making efforts to control car ownership. Beijing's belated introduction of a free lottery system has not been a success; many people who don't really need a car participate just because it's free. Consequently, the allocation ratio has fallen to around 50:1. In my view, Shanghai's auction system at least recognises that car owners should pay for the pressure they put on public infrastructure. So there's social justification for the Shanghai system. And compared with Beijing's random allocation, the Shanghai auction allows those who really need a car to buy that right.

Unfortunately, though, this serviceable system is under pressure from many different sources. Car-makers, I am sure, are among them. It has become very popular in China for leaders of public opinion to criticise the government for being excessively controlling. Ironically, though, there has been very little criticism of the latest changes in Shanghai. Self-interest – in this case, the prospect of driving more cheaply – seems to come before public interest – despite the pollution problem that Shanghai faces, of which exhaust fumes are a significant part.

Anyway, now is certainly a good time to buy cars in Shanghai – as long as you are blessed with quick fingers and nerves of steel!

A Letter From China
28 November 2013
Tony Wu

Chapter 38

How to buy an apartment in Shanghai

After I graduated from university in 2001, I bought a tiny apartment in downtown Shanghai for Rmb4,000/square metre; today, the same fiat is probably worth Rmb40,000/sqm. Unfortunately, I sold the fiat in 2004 when I went to work abroad, merely doubling my money in two years, but failed to get back on the property ladder on my return. In 2001 I was encouraged to buy a property because I only needed a 20% downpayment, and I calculated that monthly repayment of the 30-year mortgage would be roughly equal to monthly rental. Also, the tax bureau would give me a break on my income tax, and, most importantly, the government would grant me a Shanghai hukou which meant that I would become a real Shanghainese (I'm actually from Yunnan, but keep quiet about it these days).

All those favourable policies are long gone, but Shanghai property prices continue to rise because, I think, more and more people are dreaming of becoming citizens of a first-tier city in which working opportunities are abundant, educational standards are high and healthcare resources are the best in the country.

Now, the prospect of a baby has forced me back into the property market. I would have preferred to buy a smart new apartment, fully decorated. But there is little residential land in downtown Shanghai now, so as I wanted to buy a property in a good location, I had to look at the secondary market. (It may seem strange to foreigners, but we Chinese have a strong preference for new, rather than used, homes.)

So began my nine-month search. The offices of real estate agents line many streets (they disappeared in 2009, but have now returned with a vengeance). Over the nine months I contacted around 15. In retrospect this was a mistake, as I now receive about 10 cold calls every day; the agents have generously shared my mobile number with friends and colleagues. I must have visited nearly 100 properties.

The deal, when it finally came in July, was completed by the seller and me face to face in 10 minutes. I only got a 2% discount, but the stated price was reasonable. Even then, I had to fight off four estate agents trying to gazump the property. The 130sqm flat is on the 16th floor of a block built in 2003 and has three bedrooms. It is in Pudong, near the

At 8am many people are already waiting in front of the Pudong Real Estate Trading Centre

People waiting for the qualification check

Yuanshen Stadium, so not too far from work (seven minutes if traffic is good, so half an hour normally). Just as important, it is in the catchment area for a good school, Fushan Foreign Language School.

After signing the property agreement, the buyer and seller need to go to the real estate trading centre to register the transaction and issue the new property deed.

Buying a property now is nothing like 12 years ago. I remember that then it only took an hour to register the transaction and 10 days to issue the new deed. Now it at least takes a day to register and two months to issue the deed. Why is this?

The answer lies in the local government's attempts to curb property prices. In 2010 the Shanghai government disallowed non-Shanghainese citizens from buying property until they had worked over a year in the city (this was extended to two years from November 2013). Also, a

Shanghainese family can buy a maximum of two properties, with only one property allowed for a single individual. So every time you register a transaction, you need to pass through a qualification check to make sure that you are entitled to buy. The trading centre will check whether you are a Shanghai citizen, whether you are single or married, and if you are divorced how any previously held property was allocated. If they find out that you have more than the allowed number of properties under your name, you cannot buy.

Apart from the qualification check, the trading centre also needs to check the transaction price. Unlike in previous years, when the government not only charged almost zero tax but also returned the individual's income tax, the government now charges 5% business tax on the transaction price and 2% individual income tax on the

The queuing ticket shows that my number is 8155; there are only 122 people in front of me...

profit if the seller holds the property for less than five years, or 5% business tax and 1% individual income tax on the profit if the seller holds the property for more than five years. People sometimes will purposely register a lower transaction price in order to save tax, but the price is checked by the trading centre to decide whether it is fair.

If you are lucky, you can get the qualification check and price check finished within a day. If you need to provide further evidence, then you would have to set aside another day to complete this part of the process. After the checking is finished, the centre's officials accept your registration and ask you to come back in 20 working days to pay tax, after which they will process the deed transfer. And it takes another 20 working days for you to finally get the deed and close the transaction.

I was chatting with my agent when we were waiting. He is 23 years old and from Guizhou province in the southwest of China. He came to Shanghai three years ago to experience its cosmopolitan life. He earns Rmb1,600 in basic salary per month, with a monthly bonus based on his performance. His employer (in this case a Taiwanese realtor called Pacific Rehouse) charges 2% commission on the transaction price (1% each to seller and buyer); the agent himself gets 10% to 15% of the commission as a bonus. He told me that his total monthly pay averages Rmb5,000.

I sorted out my mortgage, with a 30% downpayment, from China Merchants Bank. I was lucky, as towards year-end the bank's mortgage quota gets tight. I was one of the last to get a 15% first-property buyer discount. It is a floating-rate 30-year mortgage – currently 5.75%. I also qualified for a Rmb300,000 loan at 4.5% from the Housing Fund.

So finally I got my apartment in September – what a mess! I am now embarking on decoration – but that's another story. I am quoted Rmb250,000 (roughly 5% of the apartment cost) with a finish date of March, as Chinese New Year intervenes. Friends tell me I will be lucky to come in on time and on budget ...

A Letter From China
30 November 2013
Jason Xu

Chapter 39

Memory lane

On a fine winter's afternoon earlier this week, I drove the 70 km to Jinshan. It was hardly a stroll down memory lane, as most of my journey was on a six-lane highway, but I was visiting Shanghai Petrochemical, which was the second H-share to list; it was only pipped to the post by Tsingtao Beer, because of the complexities of simultaneously issuing an ADR. Back in 1993, the company was subject to a fierce wooing by the world's leading investment banks. My colleague on this trip visited as part of the Peregrine pitch team, while I was working for Warburg (for

Abandon hope? The entrance to the Shanghai Petrochemical compound in Jinshan

younger readers, these were once flourishing banks that are now one with Nineveh and Tyre). This time I was visiting Jinshan to check out the story of an ambitious privately owned neighbour. In fact, I had been somewhat surprised to find the company still listed on Bloomberg. I thought it had been amongst the nine subsidiaries swallowed by its parent, Sinopec. But while Zhenhai, Yanshan, Qilu and Yangzijiang are no longer independent, Shanghai Petrochemical still survives. It was a near-run thing – investors twice rejected attempts at privatisation back in 2006 and 2007, balmy days in the A-share market. Judging by the current share price, they would have done better to accept.

My arrival was certainly reminiscent of former times: a guard prevented me from taking a photograph of the building (clearly a state secret) and directed me through a cavernous, under-lit marble reception area. However, the affable board secretary, helped by two young assistants, was at pains to explain to me how much the company had changed. Mr Zhang had been sent to Jinshan at the end of the Cultural Revolution and had stayed ever since, helping as the company became a model for the import of foreign technology and equipment under Deng Xiaoping's Open Door policy. Whereas at one time the company and the town were almost interchangeable, the company, like one of those before-and-after slimming adverts, is now a shadow of its former self. Before IPO, the brokers and lawyers had managed to shave 20,000 people off the payroll, so at listing the staff number was recorded as a mere 36,000. Today the official workforce is just under 15,000, and the actual workforce is 12,000 – there are more than 2,000 people on "internal retirement" who are paid 70% of their salary not to show up, as well as 1,000 people who once worked the farmland which the plant took over 40 years ago. Meanwhile, assets have tripled. Staff numbers will fall further as the company retreats from its once-profitable chemical-fibre business; one PET (polyethylene thalaphtalate) plant has been closed, and it sounds as though more will follow.

Last June the company became almost the last to complete its reform of non-tradable shares, launched in 2005 with an improved offer held to A-share holders of five additional shares for every ten. Now that the company is far from being a privatisation target, the new leadership under Chairman Fu at Sinopec views the listing status as a valuable platform. There is even a plan under discussion to establish an option scheme, the first in the Sinopec Group, by which top management would be issued options into up to 1% of the company, based on the achievement of eight targets (eight is a lucky number in China).

The company has expanded its refinery business in recent years as its chemical business has fallen into loss. Under the phase-6 expansion, the company improved its ability to process dirtier crude oil; capital spending peaked in 2013 at Rmb6.2 billion. Mr Zhang praised the new fuel-price-adjustment mechanism, introduced last March, whereby the government adjusts fuel prices every 10 days in line with international prices. The company is therefore now allowed to make $1.5 to $2.5 profit per barrel, compared with the losses of 2011/12 when, at a time of high inflation, the refiners were asked to do national service. It remains to be seen whether the government will be able to stick to the plan should inflation accelerate again. Gearing is now just over 50%. Of the company's Rmb9 billion debt, 90% is short-term and 90% of that is in US dollars. The renminbi is going up, apparently, so this is unhedged. The company is setting up an office in the new Shanghai Free Trade Zone, as this will help it to access cheap offshore finance in ways as yet unspecified.

The best view of the complex turned out to be from the men's washroom on the 14th floor. On a clear day (most common in October, apparently, and on the website www.spc.com.cn) you can see over to the 36km bridge, a modern wonder, which spans the treacherous currents of Hangzhou Bay. The largest smokestack, striped red and white, was an

Smokestack lightin'; the sun sets over Shanghai Petrochemical

oil-fired power station, now closed, to be replaced by a cheaper coal-fired one. The petrochemical park stretches for 24.9 square kilometres. Mr Zhang said that there would be no problem here in building, say, a PX (paraxylene) plant (recently rejected by the citizens of Dalian and Chengdu through street protests). Given the coming glut of shale-gas-driven plastics from the US, the company is anxious to develop speciality products, including carbon fibre (spokesmen have been telling me about carbon fibre in the same hushed tones for 20 years).

At a time when the A-share and H-share markets are overall trading pretty much in line, Shanghai Petrochemical's A-share trades at an 85% premium. In this case, I think, it is less to do with superior knowledge on the part of local investors and more to do with their speculative love of stocks with low absolute prices and asset-injection stories. Indeed, Mr Zhang spoke of the possible injection of good assets from the parent and the sale of bad assets (though he subsequently found it easier to indicate the bad assets to be ejected than the good assets to be injected). It should also be noted that the company's A-shares represent only 10% of the shares in issue, while the H-shares represent 32.4%.

It is easy to be cynical about state-owned companies. Even though the company has made progress during its listed history it is still, essentially, uninvestible. However, when you think that what the titans of finance were fighting over 20 years ago is now a mere 0.14% of the Shanghai Composite Index, and does not even qualify for the Hang Seng, you realize just how far China has come.

A Letter From China
27 January 2014
Chris Ruffle

Chapter 40

Episodes in public hospitals

An early-morning visit to the emergency room

This happened eight years ago. Life in an investment bank had taken its toll on me. Working day and night on an IPO had caused me to lose my voice. At four in the morning, I woke up with a fever. After a brief discussion, my husband and I overcame our fear of going to the emergency room of a public hospital, and went to a well-known Class III hospital (the top grade in China).

Fortunately, there were not that many people in the internal-medicine department. A nurse took my temperature and asked me to go to a small room nearby. A thirty-something doctor asked me to sit down. He was wearing a gown that was hardly white any more, though I was not sure whether the particular shade of grey was due to numerous washes or just dirt. My husband told him my symptoms, and the doctor checked my throat. "Bronchitis. IV first, and then take these medicines" he said, expressionlessly. Chinese doctors love intravenous injections. "No IV" my husband said firmly.

The doctor raised his head, looking at us, and saw in our faces that we were not open to negotiation. "OK", he said. He scribbled down several items on the prescription sheet. I could hardly read his handwriting. My husband asked what they were. He told us the names of the drugs, including a kind of cephalosporin (an antibiotic), a penicillin-type antibiotic, and a few types of Chinese medicine, including a syrup for coughing.

I was surprised to see that I needed to take so many drugs. In particular, I was irritated at the thought of having to take two antibiotics – so much so that I forgot that I had asked my husband to speak to the doctor on my behalf, given my lost voice. Instead, in a voice as low as a fly's, I asked the doctor why he had prescribed two antibiotics. He was a bit stunned by my unexpected low voice. He looked at me and asked gently, "So which one would you like to use?"

I was quite amused by his expression and his question. I felt as if I were in a market, negotiating with the seller on some goods to buy. Luckily, my brain was still functioning well enough, and I was able to

The waiting game

employ my limited medical knowledge to pick one of the antibiotics that I thought would be useful to me. On the way back home, I couldn't help regretting having made the trip to the hospital. I could simply have gone to a pharmacy to get some antibiotics of my own choosing during the day.

Eight years later, I can no longer buy antibiotics in a pharmacy without any prescription – at least not in the big cities. Nor do I think that one would get two antibiotics prescribed for a minor bacterial infection in a Class III hospital of a first-tier city. Nevertheless, over-treatment is still endemic in China.

A visit to the gynaecologist

A minor note on my physical check-up report had got me concerned. I decided to see a specialist in gynaecology. I checked the websites of the well-known Class III hospitals in Shanghai, and was glad to find that there was a public hotline I could use to make an appointment with a specialist (at director level). I immediately called the hotline. The receptionist was nice, and she went back to check the availability. It was the beginning of the month, but her answer gave me a chill: "There's nothing available for this month.

"How about next month?" I asked.

"You'll need to call back. We give out the slots for registration on the 21st of each month at 12 am. Alternatively, you could go to hospital to get a registration number. "

The queue goes ever on ...

What? Call back at midnight? No wonder there are people waiting in long lines for a registration number for a visit to a specialist in the middle of the night. I gave up. After talking to a few friends, I decided to try my luck by going to a Class II (lower than Class III) hospital early for a visit to a specialist of a lower status, an associate director. So one morning, I set off to the hospital early, and arrived there at 7 am. The doctors would start to see patients at 8:30. I had thought I was early, but there were more than 20 people in front of me. I was lucky that I could still find a small place on the bench to sit on. I waited and waited.

The whole morning passed. As I was waiting, I got worried as I saw the door to the doctor's office was halfway open most of the time. When it was my turn, I was called in and found that the previous patient was still pulling her pants on. I was embarrassed and wanted to retreat, but the doctor's firm voice asked me to sit down. The lady didn't seem to mind, and she went outside of the room as I was sitting down. I then closed the door behind me. The doctor asked me what was wrong while still looking at some document in her hand. Just after I explained my problem, and was ready to undress and lie down on the bench for the doctor's examination, someone opened the door, and several curious heads squeezed in. I was seriously irritated.

"I haven't started! Just get out!" I shouted at the heads. They disappeared.

Hearing this, the doctor looked at me, puzzled at my annoyance: "No need to be so harsh."

"Well, you should have told them that!" I forgot my manners. The doctor didn't reply, but quickly finished her examination, and told me her diagnosis and suggestion for treatment. I vaguely remember that she suggested some minimally invasive operation. But by that time, I was only thinking about escaping from the place as soon as I could. I didn't care even to ask her any more questions. It took me just around six minutes from entering the doctor's office to leaving the hospital, but the whole visit took me more than four hours. I didn't follow the doctor's advice afterwards, because later I learned that my problem did not require medical intervention after all.

After that visit, I was lucky to find a place that could offer a patient some respect as an individual. I certainly don't mind paying a great deal more to avoid that kind of experience I had at the Class II hospital!

A Letter From China
17 February 2014
Vicky Chen

Chapter 41

In the lap of the gods

This letter is not about investment but about religion. While pundits try to predict what will happen over the course of 2014, in Taiwan we simply refer matters to the gods.

In contrast to the mainland, religious beliefs have been protected in Taiwan. As a consequence, religion is flourishing on the island. According to official statistics, Taiwan has 9,422 Daoist temples and 2,348 Buddhist temples. That's one temple for every 1,954 people. (There are also 3,274 churches, mostly Presbyterian, and only 25 Confucian temples, but we are going to concentrate on the traditional religions in this letter).

As the numbers imply, you can easily find a temple when you walk around a Taiwanese city. Polytheism is the defining characteristic: among the more commonly occurring gods, we have the Jade Emperor, the head of deities; celestial masters, of whom the most common is Laozi (Lao-tzu), the writer of the classic Dao De Jing (Tao Te Ching); and many different subsidiary deities: the Dragon King, in charge of the oceans, Yanluo, the king of hell, and the popular Mazu, a mortal-turned-goddess who has been saving people from disasters since the Song Dynasty.

The government takes the gods seriously: President Ma Ying-jeou has signed this banner honouring Mazu's kindness in protecting people.

Let's go to a popular Mazu temple to find out how to ask the deity any questions you might have. On entering a temple, you must first burn incense sticks to send your greetings to its presiding deities. Usually, the temple will give you instructions as to how many incense sticks you should light. The incense sticks are supplied free of charge in Taiwanese temples (on the Chinese mainland, you have to pay for them). Of course, you can donate money to demonstrate your sincerity. To save trouble for believers without a lighter (a growing problem as the number of smokers falls), a stove is provided to burn the incense sticks.

After greeting the deities in the temples, you need to get some divination chips. These croissant-shaped wooden objects have two sides, one flat one convex. Once cast, the combinations provide different answers: one positive (flat side up) with one negative (convex side up) means that the deity answers your question positively, a "yes": the probability is 0.5. Two positive chips mean that what you asked is not clear, that or the gods smile at what you said: the probability is 0.25; you have to ask again. Two negative chips means that what you asked for is denied, a "no": the probability is 0.25.

Hold the chips, circle them above the incense burner to "clean" them, then kneel down in front of the gods' statues to state who you are, when you were born, where you live and what you want to ask. A tip: only ask one question when casting the chips, so as not to confuse the gods.

Picking up a pair of divination chips

Once you receive a "yes", you draw a bamboo divination straw, then come back to ask if the straw is right. You have to go for another straw until a throw of the chips shows a "yes". There are usually 60 straws with different predictions: good, neutral or bad. You can then find the Chinese poem indicated by the "Yes" straw and read its explanation for different fields such as business, health, finding lost items, pregnancy, marriage, love, lawsuits, reputation, and even the weather. If you can't understand clearly, the senior staff in the temple can explain it to you. You can express your appreciation to the gods by sending fruit, burning paper money, donating money or gold, or even playing movies or theatre in front of the deities' statues. Or you can simply give thanks with all your heart.

Drawing the straws is a purely random event from a scientific point of view. But when I brought my wife, her cousin and a Chinese friend to cast straws in two different temples on two separate days, three of the four straws were the same, even though we asked different questions. The probability is 46 million to one. The lucky matching slips are called ren xu,

Straw poll

in which ren represents the river and xu means the mountain, one combination of the "60 heavenly stems and earthly branches" (an ancient Chinese calendar system). The poetry means that like a lonely light to brighten a dark night, you can have the gods' blessing if you are silently spreading kindness.

You are, of course, welcome to visit Taiwan to ask how your investments for the future stack up!

Note: Open Door does not use divination in determining stock selection for its funds. Nor do Confucian temples ….

A Letter From Taiwan
17 February 2014
Warren Lin

Chapter 42

Going underground

I've always liked maps. The map of the London underground is a classic. It might not have the exotic appeal of an atlas page of the Malaysian archipelago, but it has the benefit of everything being eminently reachable. All I needed to do was to stay on the train to enjoy the delights of Theydon Bois, Burnt Oak or Cockfosters; I never did (fortunately, I am sure, for my illusions) but I might have. There are also the Tube's interesting kinks and complexities – how on earth do you get to Mornington Crescent?

So in my travels around China, I have taken a more than passing interest in its metro systems. There are now plenty to choose from. There was a long hiatus after Beijing opened its first line in 1971, but from the commencement of Shanghai's system in 1995 and Taipei's in 1996, the tunnel builders have been kept busy. There are, at the last count, 20 Chinese cities with metros, and a further couple of dozen at various stages in the construction or approval process. Wuxi, Changsha and Ningbo are all due to open systems this year. Even Urumqi in the far northwest is due to open one in 2016. The latest statistics show a total track length of 2,575 km carrying 33 million passengers per day.

Beijing still leads in terms of scale with 17 lines, 232 stations, 465 km of track and a ridership capacity of 3.2 billion per year. Shanghai has more track (538 km and still expanding) and more stations (329) but lower

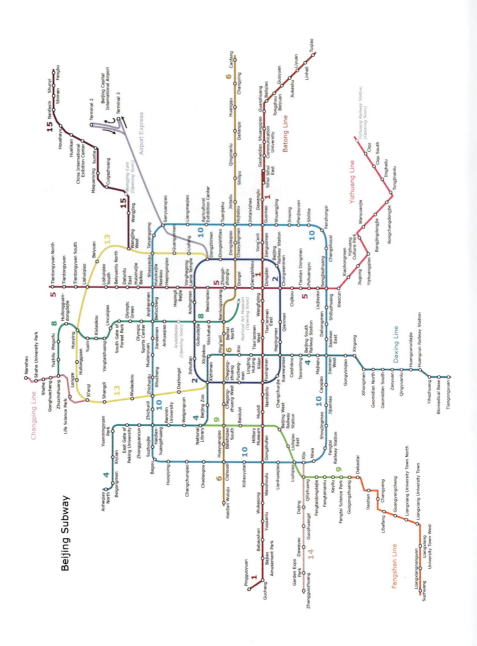

Beijing Subway

Going underground

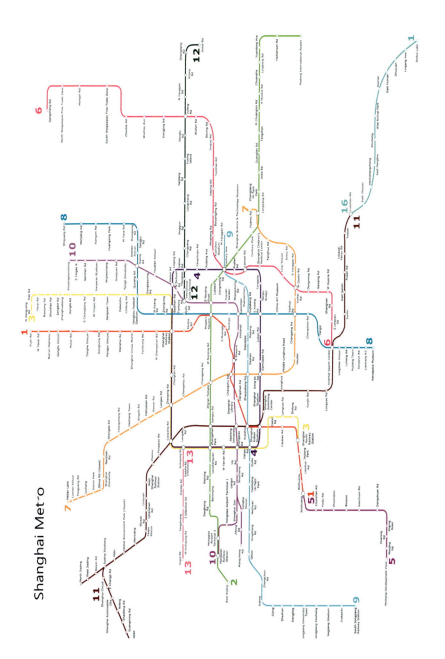

Shanghai Metro

ridership (2.5 billion). To put this in context, the venerable London Tube has a ridership of 1.2 billion. The map of the Beijing system bears a more than passing resemblance to London's with an east–west Line 1 like the Central Line and a circular Line 2. The fact that many of the station names on Line 2 end in men or "gate" reveals that the track follows the line of the old city walls, demolished by Mao to make way for the first ring road. Other characters with a high occurrence in stations names are gong (palace), qiao (bridge) and jing (well). Note the slightly sinister comment that the station at the Military Museum is currently closed.

Shanghai's system is built around the east–west (Line1) and north–south (Line 2) axis. These lines cross at People's Square. It is difficult to believe that there can be any busier station; it handles 400,000 passengers a day. I strongly advise anyone with a tendency to claustrophobia to avoid the corridor linking the two lines at rush hour. Shanghai's system is less compact than Beijing's, with long arms stretching out across the flat plain to distant industrial suburbs and dormitory towns. The characteristic of Shanghai's station names is that they feature the names of many other cities in China, a result of Communist officials' sudden need to come up with new street names to replace the colonial originals in 1949.

Most of the other systems are simple east–west/north–south arrangements in the shape of a cross; Xi'an, Suzhou, Shenyang and Chengdu all follow this pattern. Kunming's subway should be cross-shaped, but the lines don't yet meet in the middle (Kunming has not been overly blessed with talented town planners). Some of the cities face geographical challenges – perhaps none more so than Chongqing, where the old city centre is like the prow of a ship between two steep-sided rivers.

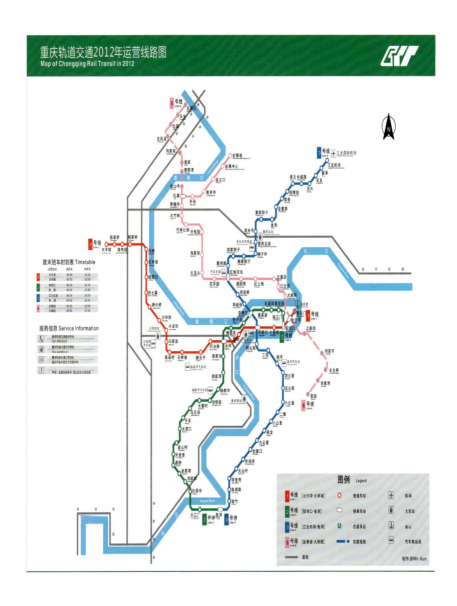

The systems of Guangzhou and Foshan have grown so that they now join up, as would Shenzhen's and Hong Kong's, were they allowed to do so. Shenzhen's system has the boast of the highest station density (137 on only 178 km of track); the council clearly had difficulty in saying no. The simplest system at the moment belongs to Harbin (one line of 17 km with 18 stations) though the Harbinese are no less proud of it.

With huge and growing urban populations, affordable mass transit is clearly a priority in China, and one which the petrol lobby has not been able to undermine. The underground is a cheap way to travel here. The cheapest, oddly, is Beijing, where journeys of any length cost just Rmb2. The most expensive trip in Shanghai is Rmb15. The cheapness of the metro, combined with traffic jams above ground, now make the service popular with courier companies, where a representative outside the barrier hands parcels to a representative inside. Perhaps in acknowledgement of Chinese customers' creativity, the system is stingy in offering volume discounts, such as monthly or season passes.

Finally, the Taipei system deserves a specific mention, with passengers queuing in orderly fashion along white lines painted on the platform, in contrast to the every-man-for-himself scramble which is the norm for boarding rush-hour trains in mainland China. My limited use of the system also indicated above-average adherence to the laws governing the use of the special seats reserved for senior citizens or parents with children. Taipei's station names show a high occurrence of the character shan or "mountain", by which the city is surrounded. From personal experience, I can assure readers that some of the end-of-the-line stations are actually places worth visiting. Maokong, Tamsui and Beitou are all preferable, I would suggest, to Cockfosters.

A Letter From China
18 February 2014
Chris Ruffle

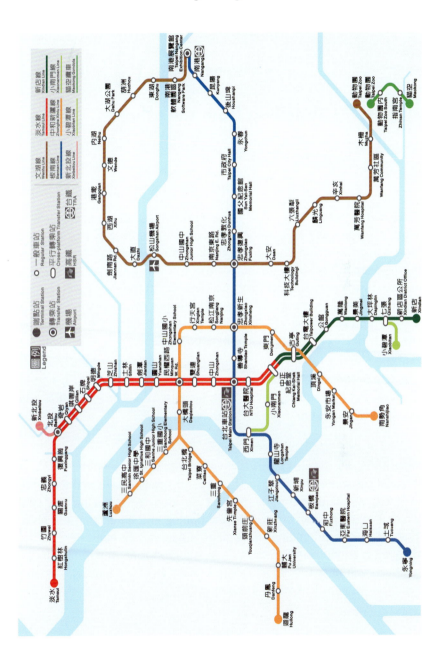

Chapter 43

Retailing from the ashes

Songshan Cigarette Factory in Taipei has an incendiary history. It was established in 1937 as a monopoly tobacco producer by the colonial Japanese government, in order to supply not only the domestic market but also Japan's growing offshore empire. It was a symbol of Taiwan's industrialisation, with advanced facilities – dormitories, shower rooms, medical care, pharmacy, surgery and even a kindergarten – for its 1,200 employees. Just 10 years later, on 28 February 1947, it was the site of a riot against the heavy-handed occupation of the island by the Kuomintang forces, which sought over-vigorously to enforce this valuable monopoly. The factory generated revenue of NT$21 billion at its peak, but was shut down in 1988 because of urban expansion and mounting competition from offshore brands.

Now, ironically, the old factory is covered with signs prohibiting smoking (Taiwan has some of the most rigorous anti-smoking laws in the world). In 2002, the Taipei city government decided to redevelop the site, which is close to the smart Hsinyi shopping and entertainment area. The old Japanese buildings have been preserved on eight hectares of the site as an innovation centre and exhibition zone; the remaining 10 hectares will host the Taipei Dome ("Giant Egg" in Chinese), a multi-function stadium scheduled to open in 2017.

Eslite, Taiwan's leading bookstore chain, recently opened a store and hotel on the site. Eslite has a history of retail innovation; in 1999 its branch store in Dunhua Road was the first one to operate round the clock, and the company gained an "Asia Best" award from Time magazine in 2004 for its attractive design. Under increasing pressure from the internet, and with narrowing margins, the bookstore gradually developed as a loss-leader to attract young people, from whom money can be made via fashion boutiques and restaurants on other floors. This is the design of Eslite's flagship store in Hsinyi. The new store in the Songshan Cigarette Factory takes the concept one step further. Books, music, high-end food stalls and fashion are now mixed together on one floor, and indeed in one display. There is even a display of music on old vinyl LPs, together with the turntables on which to play them; all achingly cool. When you can buy almost anything more cheaply and conveniently online, shopping becomes entirely about the experience. Shops must be fun places to visit and hang out in. On my visit to this bookstore, I came away with more food than books.

Whereas China used to be a late copier of Western retail models, it is interesting to see such innovation developing here. Perhaps in a future letter I will tell you about Ultraviolet, voted Shanghai's best restaurant, which does not even have an address, serves only 10 people each night, and accompanies each course with an audio-visual display to enhance the taste ...

A Letter From Taiwan
21 March 2014
Warren Lin

Chapter 44

The rules of the (Chinese) road

In this book we seek to show what China is really like today, not how it is presented. For those wanting to know the official, voluminous traffic rules in China, there are perfectly good websites (www.110.com or http://kaoshi.jxedt.com). The following are the 12 rules that actually apply, as derived from several years of observation:

Buses have right of way

1. The larger vehicle always has right of way.

2. Especially when it is a bus or a coal lorry.

3. SUVs take precedence over other passenger cars (being cut up by an attractive lady driving a Porsche Carrera is a common feature of driving in the swankier parts of Shanghai).

4. Pedestrians have no right of way, even when there are stripy lines on the road or a flashing green man. On no account yield to a pedestrian unless overwhelmed by numbers.

5. When the lights change and you are turning left, see if you can be the last vehicle to squeeze across in front of the oncoming traffic.

6. If the lights change and the car in front of you does not immediately move away, honk your horn loudly. This is obligatory.*

7. On no account catch the eye of another driver or pedestrian. If you are looking in a different direction, it is the other man's fault.

8. If you have an accident, do not pull over to the side of the road. Stay exactly where you are until the police arrive to confirm your insurance claim. When this happens at rush hour, on a busy intersection or in the rain (the most productive time for a prang), you may get some dirty looks from drivers filing past at a snail's pace. Either a.) ignore them or b.) entertain them with a shouting match or fight.

9. There is always room for one more lane of traffic, whatever the lines on the road might indicate.

10. When the car's number plate shows that it comes from another province, give it a wide berth. The driver is lost and liable to make a wild manoeuvre when his GPS suddenly finds a road it recognises.

11. Be careful when overtaking or cutting in front of black cars with red characters on the number plate. These are more frequent in Beijing (lots of embassies) and the cities where the commands of the seven military regions are located: Beijing, Guangzhou, Kunming, Nanjing, Lanzhou, Chengdu and Shenyang.**

12. For mopeds, all rules are optional (red lights, one way streets, sidewalks etc.).

Newer models use airbags

*On an evening flight back from Chengdu, I sat next to a Swedish engineer working for the local Volvo JV. In a jocular spirit I suggested they must have to strengthen the horns on the Chinese versions of their cars. They do! The engineer gave me a detailed explanation of exactly how.

**Note: a red WJ stands for wujing or "military police".

A Letter From China
21 March 2014
Chris Ruffle

Chapter 45

Take the day off

You can tell a lot about a country from the holidays it takes. China's holidays traditionally revolve around the agricultural calendar. The long lunar New Year holiday takes place when there's the least to do in the fields. The mid-autumn festival on the 15th day of the eighth month takes place in late September or early October and coincides with the end of the harvest when a full moon will illuminate the celebrations. The accompanying moon-cake tradition derives, apparently, from the Sung dynasty (note: these cakes are primarily intended as gifts, and I cannot recommend eating them: they have more calories than a Ben & Jerry's ice cream, but can taste like stale Christmas pudding). The festival of Qingming (literally "pure bright") occurs on the 15th day after the spring equinox and is traditionally devoted to visiting your ancestors' tombs and giving them a spring clean. Apparently it was introduced by the Tang emperor Xuanzong in 732 AD, in order to reduce extravagant funeral rites by confining ceremonies to the area of the tomb itself – an earlier version of Xi Jinping's anti-conspicuous consumption campaign. We got our Qingming in early this year because on the actual day the cemeteries are a mob scene. The Dragon Boat or Duanwu festival occurs at the summer solstice; there are various explanations given to the traditions of boat racing and eating zongzi (rice dumplings steamed in leaves much better than mooncakes). The most popular is that this represents people taking boats out onto the Miluo River where the poet and patriot Qu Yuan had drowned himself (circa 278 BC) and throwing the zongzi into the river to distract the fishes from eating his body. In Jiangsu, however, the suicide is Wu Zixu (died 484 BC), while in Zhejiang it's a girl called Cao E (died 143 AD), drowned searching for her father.

The Mid-autumn, Qingming and Dragon Boat festivals have continued uninterrupted in Taiwan and Hong Kong, but were only revived in the People's Republic in 2008. This is when the PRC dropped a long Labour Day holiday in May, established in 2000 in emulation of Japan's "Golden Week", as the authorities began to realize that giving such a vast population a public holiday on the same day is a recipe for traffic chaos. Lunar New Year, when families traditionally return to their hometowns, is already the planet's largest human migration. An attempt this year to try to shorten the New Year holiday by excluding New Year's Eve was not well received, however, and seems likely to be reversed. The other long holiday is National Day in October, celebrating the establishment of the PRC on 1 October 1949. This is usually an excuse for China's leaders to wear Mao jackets and wave at tanks in Tiananmen Square. It had somewhat fallen out of fashion in recent years, but may be revived given the new belligerence in China's foreign policy. In total China has 17 days of

public holiday, putting it well up the public-holiday charts alongside other pace-setters such as Egypt and Portugal. This perhaps reflects the relatively low level of non-statutory holidays given to workers in China.

Taiwan, in contrast, only has 10 days of public holiday. In addition to the traditional holidays described above, Taiwan used to celebrate Confucius' birthday (and mine) as Teacher's Day on 28 September. Unfortunately for Confucius, Taiwan's first elected president, Lee Teng Hui, in 1995 moved this holiday to 28 February, to commemorate an anti-government rising which took place on that day in 1947 against the occupying forces of KMT governor Chen Yi, who had mishandled the takeover from the surrendering Japanese. Thousands (estimates vary widely) died in the subsequent "White Terror". Chen Yi himself was executed in 1950, but not because of incompetence; he was suspected of being about to defect. Taiwan's own national day is 10 October. This is not, as one might have guessed, the anniversary of the founding of the Republic of China (which took place on 1 January 1912) but marks the start of the Wuchang Uprising. This was a half-baked coup by New

Army units stationed in Wuhan; not ready for the intended launch date at the mid-autumn festival, rebellion was eventually forced upon the conspirators by the accidental explosion of a bomb at their HQ. Fireworks are a key feature of all Chinese festivities (together with lots of food and drink). At the slightest excuse the Chinese will light the blue touch paper (see chapter entitled Big Bangs). One of the most spectacular displays takes place in Taipei on the Double Tenth (10 October). A prime position for watching it is the Grand Hotel, in front of which is displayed a flag of all the countries that still recognize the Republic of China. In between fireworks, I spent my time trying to guess which they are; how well can you do? (answers on the back page – I scored 2!)

It is surprising how many military disasters are commemorated. 1 August, Army Day in the PRC, marks the Nanchang Uprising in 1927, the first Communist battle against the KMT, featuring a youthful Zhou Enlai and Soviet advisors, in which the nascent PLA was soundly defeated. This is not actually a "public" holiday in that only the army gets a holiday (not all of them, one hopes). The same applies to Women's Day, Children's Day and Youth Day (on 4 May, to mark the student protests in 1919 against Japan's gains in the Treaty of Versailles

– this also was not terribly successful). Single's Day (11 November – work it out) is a recent invention which has become a kind of Valentine's Day on steroids under the tutelage of China's powerful e-commerce sector; online transactions totalled Rmb45 billion on this day alone in 2013. As there is no cost to such holiday-less holidays, the government is free to invent new ones at will, such as the recent gratuitous establishment of 3 September to mark victory in the war against Japanese aggression and 13 December to commemorate the Nanjing Massacre. There are additionally some Tibetan and Muslim holidays that apply only in the west and which we don't talk about very much.

For such a hard-working place, Hong Kong does well for public holidays (14 in total) because it adds the normal Christian festivals on top of the traditional Chinese ones. It even celebrates Chinese holidays not taken in the PRC or Taiwan, such as Buddha's Birthday on the eighth day of the fourth month, and the Double Ninth or Double Yang festival on the ninth day of the ninth month. As there is too much yang around on this day, Hong Kongers are meant to drink chrysanthemum tea and climb to the top of a tall mountain (not sure about the second of these, but the tea's not bad) Hong Kong also gets to celebrate the founding of itself as a "semiautonomous region" on 1 July.

In the past these holidays have really only affected people living in, or visiting, China, or, as an investor, when you hear that the China markets are going to be closed on such and such a day. But with the coming boom in overseas travel by the Chinese, foreigners may need to take more note of Chinese holidays. And get the fireworks ready.

A Letter From China
11 April 2014
Chris Ruffle

1. Burkina Faso
2. Dominican Republic
3. Saint Vincent and the Grenadines
4. Solomon Islands
5. Marshall Islands
6. Guatemala
7. Belize
8. Panama
9. Honduras
10. Kiribati
11. Paraguay
12. Nicaragua
13. Palau
14. El Salvador
15. Nauru
16. Saint Lucia
17. São Tomé
18. Saint Kitts and Nevis
19. Holy See
20. Haiti
21. Tuvalu
22. Swaziland

Chapter 46

Innovations in ice cream

"You mean that I have to queue an hour for an ice cream? You have to be kidding?" And it wasn't as if I was in some fancy establishment in Taipei; this was in laid-back Taichung. Still, the ice creams being eaten around me looked very good, and I had nowhere else I needed to be, so I shrugged and took my turn in the queue.

A ruin reborn: the building formerly known as Miyahara Eye Clinic

Miyahara Eye Clinic: an unusual name for an ice-cream brand

The building itself is interesting. Dawncake, a specialist in cheese and pineapple cakes, acquired this abandoned building in 2010. Inscribed on the stone portal are the characters "Miyahara Eye Clinic". This was founded by Takekuma Miyahara in 1927, when Taiwan was a Japanese colony (1895–1945). After the war things went downhill and the building's subsequent uses included hair salon, eatery, taxi bureau, bus station and newspaper office. It was finally ruined by the big 921 earthquake in 1999 and further damaged by Typhoon Kalmaegi in 2008, becoming a dangerous building requiring demolition. Dawn rescued the building, keeping the old ruins but enhancing them with an interesting new structure and decoration. From 2012, Miyahara has been reborn as a new ice-cream store; it no longer cures your eyes but satisfies your senses and stomach.

Let me show you how long the queue was outside Miyahara. By the time you get to the front, of course, you order the biggest ice cream on the menu.

I don't want you to get the wrong idea about my leisure activities, but I also visited another interesting new ice creamery in Nantou.* Nantou is a county in the mountainous centre of Taiwan with a population of about 500,000, famous for its beautiful Sun Moon Lake. This is where President Chiang Kai-shek liked to spend his down time (his house is now the five-star Lalu Hotel and the site of a Taiwan conference we organized in 2009). From these bucolic surroundings has emerged the e-commerce chocolate-maker 18 Degree Chocolate (http://www.feeling18c.com/en/). Before you ask, 18°C is the best temperature at which to taste chocolate (it's a bit like the coffee chain we used to invest in, 85°C, which, as you can doubtless guess, is the best temperature at which to make coffee.) The physical store allows passers-by to enjoy their delicious chocolate and take-away ice cream, with a rest area (to recover from the calorie intake) and free all-you-can-drink coffee and tea.

All the products are hand-made. The chocolate is wonderful, but now I think I prefer their ice cream, which comes in many novel flavours such as Lichee Rose, Black Sesame, Vegetables and Fruits, Honey Mustard and even one with salt. I wanted to try them all but they wouldn't fit in one cup.

Just right: ice cream at 18 degrees

*Note to worried readers: I am rake thin and can eat as much ice cream as I like with no discernable effect.

A Letter From China
21 March 2014
Warren Lin

Chapter 47

Ghost town

You will all have seen reports on China's "ghost town" developments. The accompanying photographs usually show a bicyclist or farmer with a hoe in front of acres of empty high-rise apartments and vacant shopping malls. The story has been a favourite filler in the Western press for some years. The most frequently cited "ghost town" is Kangbashi New Town, near the coal-rich but water-poor city of Ordos in Inner Mongolia. In recent years, the list has extended to places such as Chenggong at Kunming and Tianducheng, a replica of Paris, in Hangzhou. And in the past few weeks, there has been plenty of talk of slowing property sales, a piling up of housing inventories and falling property prices. So what do the ghost towns look like today?

China builds excellent models. Shame about the project names...

I started my trip from Changzhou, about 165 miles from Shanghai. I had decided to take an early-morning train. I boarded the high-speed train at a quarter past seven, and it arrived at five past eight. That's nice, I said to myself. But it took another 30 minutes in a taxi to reach the new district of Wujing, where the projects I was visiting are located.

The first project I visited was Le Leman City developed by the Top Spring Group. It is a massive development with aggregate gross floor area (GFA) of about one million square metres, comprising residential flats and commercial facilities, including a luxury hotel. Once completed, the project should accommodate 7,000 families. When the first phase was launched in 2007, the average price was around Rmb3,000 per square metre. There are a few blocks on sale at present, and the average offer price is Rmb6,400 per square metre. The developer told us that most of the finished flats have been sold, but that the overall occupancy rate was about 65%.

What does the buyer get for his money? I soon discovered. The garden surrounding the buildings was quite nice. What surprised me, though, was the interior. It was just bare load-bearing walls, without even internal partitions. The developer told us that the interior walls were usually knocked down by homeowners when they decorated their flats, anyway, so there was no point building them in the first place! That's right – all your money buys is a framed floor space.

I moved on to the next project, Magnolia Square, developed by the Greentown Group. This is a mega-development with a total GFA of 1.5 million square metres, which is going to accommodate about 10,000 households. Greentown is well known for its building quality and usually sells its property at a premium to its peers in the local market. The first phase of this project was on sale at an average price of Rmb7,500 per square metre. As I passed through the construction site to see the show flats, I was again impressed by the gardening works. There was even a swimming pool. But do ghosts swim, I wondered. On leaving, I noticed a couple taking wedding shots on the site (see the picture overleaf). Clearly, one person's ghost house is another's dream home.

During lunch with some local property developers, concerns were raised that in many cities there are unoccupied flats, unlet shops and empty office blocks. Were industry participants worried?

Although our local developers acknowledged the decline of sales in the first quarter and were cautious about the market outlook this year, their view of the "ghost town" phenomenon differed from the popular perception. They argued that because of the fast development of new towns and their lack of proper infrastructure and living amenities, the occupancy of new residential properties in some new districts was temporarily low. But as time passes and facilities develop, occupancy picks up. One of the speakers saw from my name card that I am based in Shanghai. "If you visited Pudong 10 years ago," he said, "even Lianyang Community could be called a ghost town. Today it is a heavily populated area."

He is right. I remember, a few years ago, a British-themed development in Songjiang, a suburb of Shanghai, called Thames Town (China's architects and developers have yet to find a new Chinese style and fall easily into pastiche). This was dubbed a ghost town in the press, but the situation is very different today. But that's in Shanghai, of course. As new districts and high-rise apartment blocks mushroom in many second- and third-tier cities, I doubt that all these developments have been carefully planned with due consideration of market demand. Over a decade of double-digit economic growth in urban China has

been forgiving of the "build it and they will come" method of property development.

The next stop was the spectacularly weird Tianducheng in the Yuhang district of Hangzhou. This development is known as the "Replica of Paris", including its very own Eiffel Tower (see picture above).

After a two-and-a-half-hour bus ride, we arrived at Paris-en-Zhejiang. Strolling through the completed residential blocks, we met only a few babies with their grandparents. It was very quiet. The shops on the ground floor were mostly unlet and locked. On the other side, however, there are still vast constructions underway.

I went into the sales office and talked to the site manager. She told me that when fully developed this satellite town would have a total GFA of about 4.5 million square metres to accommodate around 100,000 residents. Currently, only a third of the site has been developed or is under construction. When the first arrondissements were launched in 2001, properties were sold at about Rmb2,500 per square metre. Properties currently on sale have an average price of Rmb8,000 per square metre.

Questions on occupancy were dismissed: "What we care about," she said, "are sales, and more than 80% of properties launched have been sold so far." She knew why this question was asked: "I know that some media reported this project as a ghost town, and I saw the pictures taken by journalists. They take shots under the iron tower, together with a few people farming on the idle land." She continued as I tried not to smile: "But actually, the idle land was planned as a town square for commercial facilities. We are going to build it in the last stage. It has been left idle temporarily, and we allow our homeowners to farm on it for fun. You can go to see with your own eyes." She seemed a little impatient.

We walked out into the aforementioned square, surrounded by residential blocks with the large Eiffel tower sitting proudly in the middle. The land was idle, with grass growing in wild profusion. Here and there, some sections were planted with vegetables and cereal crops. As some of the homeowners were actually farmers before they lost their land and moved into flats, it is no surprise that they have planted vegetables on the spare land.

I left the so-called ghost town before night fell, in order to meet a few local bankers, trust managers and other vampires for dinner in downtown Hangzhou. It took about 45 minutes to drive into the city centre.

One manager from Bank of China told us that his bank has not intentionally tightened lending to the property sector this year, in terms of either project loans to developers or mortgage loans to homebuyers. The bank perceived mortgage loans as low-risk and low-return assets. As mortgage loans are usually conditional on a 30% to 50% downpayment, the banker was not too concerned about homebuyers walking away from their mortgages.

Trust managers also seemed to be comfortable with the loans they have granted to developers. The reason given was that trust companies have developers' properties under construction as collateral, with the loan-to-value ratio usually set at about 50%. The managers believe that if developers have liquidity problems, they can sell properties to the market and get their money back, even if they have to cut prices by 30%.

So far then, the parties involved in this great Chinese building boom are putting on a brave face. But what happens as economic growth slows? The market does not lack demand, as China's process of urbanisation continues. But this demand has been distorted by a number of factors. Flawed financial incentives for local governments and developers are a big part of the problem; chronically underfunded local authorities are dependent on the proceeds of big land sales to developers, and the officials involved have extracted benefits from the process. (On one project visit I was told I could not look at the block with the best view as it was "reserved for officials".) Behaviours are likely to change with the inevitable rollout of a recurring, rates style property tax. The poor planning of citizen services and amenities have also created many problems.

In addition, China's emerging middle class is perhaps too comfortable investing in real estate. With high savings, and limited investment options, people often buy apartments in incomplete communities, merely expecting capital values to rise, or with the vague notion that they, or some relative, will live there someday. The consequence is a string of empty and deteriorating developments that remain speculative investments rather than real homes. As the level of leverage is low, this seems unlikely to result in a Western-style property crash. But for individual investors, the return on such property may prove insubstantial – indeed ghostly.

A Letter From China
21 May 2014
Wang Zhufeng

Chapter 48

An American on the Wall

Eventually the long urban valley began to slope upwards; foothills yielded to more impressive mountain scenery and less smog. However, this was an important transport artery north from Beijing and not a place to relax; large numbers of overloaded trucks navigated the mountain tunnels amid breakdowns and varieties of self-imposed chaos. Then I saw it for the first time. I quickly pressed my face against the taxi window but was frustrated by the hills themselves, as well as by oncoming traffic and

How are your calf muscles feeling today?

nightfall. Random sections of stone and structure appeared and disappeared tantalizingly.

This, my first visit to China, was to attend an investment conference, sited eccentrically in this remote valley. It seemed to be well attended, and there were many pressing items about China's economic travails to discuss. But after a full morning's work, I was able to slip off to explore further. A short trail at the edge of the hotel grounds took me up into the lightly forested hills, and past a sign in Mandarin characters with a stern "No Entry" translation included. After a short ascent I turned a corner and there, through some foliage, found myself standing at the base of a gigantic wall.

I was confused. The path seemed to end with no direction indicated. I stood for a moment staring at the thirty-foot-high cliff of stone. With no entrance in sight I set out along the edge of the wall. As I moved along its northern side, I found myself wondering what these stones might have witnessed through the ages – wars, weather, invading Mongol armies ... I may as well have been reading in Braille as my fingertips felt the stones and my feet carried me forward.

With clouds yielding to blue skies, a light wind, an early afternoon sun and no one in sight, I made my way along the wall. Climbing upward, I stopped for a moment to reflect upon the "Do Not Enter" sign and the closed iron gate before me. Although I don't consider myself an avid climber, I enjoyed Appalachian hikes as a boy. A school trip to Teotihuacan in Mexico allowed me to climb the Pyramids of the Sun and Moon and wonder at their construction. I also once surreptitiously scaled one of the Great Pyramids in Egypt at sundown to gaze across at the Sphinx. Modern towers also draw me; I remember the World Trade Center on a humid summer day with mosquitoes sticking to the outside of glass on the 110th floor as New York City hustled below, unaware of the approaching aeroplanes. Add in bird's-eye views from the Eiffel Tower and Sacre Coeur, as well as the leaning tower of Pisa and you can detect a trend.

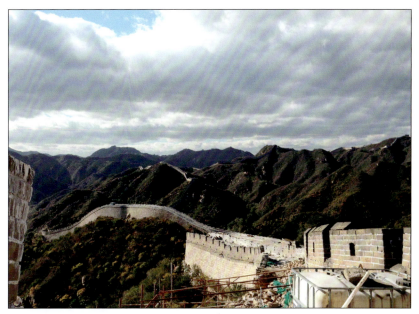

Still under construction

As I had long ago discounted the idea of tackling Everest, and with no pending trips to Dubai, my one remaining bucket-list climb now lay before me. Do you suppose I had any intention of turning back? Alas, the iron gate at the edge of the section of stone seemed to end the adventure prematurely. However, a closer inspection revealed that the gate was not locked, which in turn caused internal conflict, a particularly difficult one for a compliance officer: was it OK to go through? Did someone forget to turn the lock today? Was this a trap for the unwary (particularly those who might soon find their inability to speak Mandarin a considerable legal handicap)? No – I was supposed to go through. The gate was pushed aside on its rusty hinges and closed again, leaving me inside alone on top of the wall.

The most striking part of my walk along the Great Wall was not just the fact that the sun had shown itself. Nor was it the juxtaposition of this inspiring place far above the mountain pass with the traffic that crawled and beeped its way northward along the road a few miles below. Nor was it even the majestic and gigantic nature of the wall itself. No. The oddest thing was that, after days of bustling crowds, I was completely alone. For more than an hour I walked along, first at a very steep and determined clip upwards to the tower I had glimpsed earlier. At times I had to proceed on all fours when sudden changes in height caused new paths and

What would YOU do?

structures in the wall to appear, some of which were built out of topographic necessity and some very likely strategic. When I reached the top, I could see hill after hill receding into the distance. Fortunately, no one was there to see my jaw drop open, as I realized that each of the hills held another section of the Great Wall, which were all strung together in an incredible snaking pattern to the horizon. My camera phone does not do it justice, but I tried.

Now I was a Mongolian general. Would my armies have attacked here, or perhaps instead over by that next section down below? Where was the weak point in the wall? Was there even a weak point in this colossal structure? Or perhaps the Chinese had just left the gate open ...

An hour or so later I finally saw someone else. Actually, it was three folks out in the afternoon sun who were labouring over some supplies outside the wall's southern side together with their horses. I was still unclear about whether or not I was even supposed to be out here, and with my limited language skills I felt it might be better to avoid meeting anyone and trying to explain. I was, however, terribly curious about what they were doing. I had noted a few sections of wall along the way where some fresh masonry seemed to have been placed, and a few broken areas as well, and as I looked closer I noted that they seemed to be responsible for repairs. Of course – the friendly local repair crew! I resisted the urge to let them know that they had just a bit more work to do, secretly watched their labour for a while, and then finally turned around to enjoy the walk back. Eventually, with the sun heading down for the evening, I took a few more panoramic pirouettes and set off downhill. Truly a special experience.

A Letter From China
17 June 2014
Geoffrey Moore

Chapter 49

An American takes the train

Where would you like to go today?

I have a love-hate relationship with trains. My daily commute in San Francisco often takes about an hour, and the scenery has become overly familiar. But in a foreign country with a day of exploration ahead, it is another matter. Having heard that China's airlines leave a bit to be desired, and wishing to see as much ground as possible, I decided to take the train from my conference in Beijing to our office in Shanghai. I set out early. I had a long day in front of me, and the problems of communication were daunting. I had prepared in advance with a few classes, but was severely challenged when it was time to seek out basic amenities such as food, let alone cross-country transportation. I quickly was able to use "hello" and "thank you" to good effect, and the phrase "I don't speak Mandarin, do you speak English?" seemed as though it would be handy. However, long, detailed and fast Mandarin responses naturally tended to yield to halting confusion upon the realisation that I really did mean exactly what I said.

To the credit of the Chinese people I encountered, I was in fact able to find folks with adequate English skills. No doubt this was partly because I was traveling in large urban areas, but also is a testament to the Chinese educational system. I am willing to bet that the percentage of Chinese citizens who speak English is far in excess of those native English speakers who speak Mandarin. I have observed an increasing

A long walk in a long station

interest in learning Chinese in the US, but I suspect that this is due in part to my location in San Francisco rather than a broader American disposition. Everyone that I tried to communicate with was polite to the lost foreigner, which was refreshing when big-city impatience might have been expected. On a couple of occasions the help that I received from strangers was inspiring. It is one thing to gesture wildly and point to this train or that, but it is another when the person helps you buy your ticket and then walks you through a large station to ensure you are on the right track. In one case – my important early-morning connection out of the foothills north of Beijing – I was encouraged to run through the station as the last passengers boarded the departing train. I was late because of my taxi from the hotel. You know you are in trouble, whatever the country, when your taxi driver keeps pulling over to ask random road-walkers for directions to the only station in the vicinity. My dictionary waving was to little avail, but the buffer I had left in my schedule (I am a risk manager, after all) proved just sufficient. As I finally settled into my first Chinese train I took a deep breath. Am I on the right train? Why do we seem to be riding in the wrong direction (or am I just holding my map wrong)?

As the foothills receded and urban sprawl thickened, I became confident that I would soon be in the northern section of downtown Beijing. Some sights are the same along any train track – factories, dilapidated homes, discarded debris, people going about their daily labours. This was as comforting to my urban eye as the appearance of signs in a different language was unsettling. Gigantic buildings heralded our arrival. I studied my map further and departed the train. I was trying to travel lightly, but my baggage slowed me down as I traversed the station. Eventually, with more help from friendly and curious locals, I figured out ticketing and made my way to another train, which took me through Beijing to the south side of the city and another gigantic station. After a stop for lunch (my pronunciation of "chicken" was correct, helped perhaps by my mime), I was able to catch an earlier bullet train to Shanghai.

Hurtling forward above the ground while traveling at 300 km an hour certainly provides an interesting perspective on a foreign land. There was plenty of open land, semi-industrial or dedicated to farming. However, I was also struck by the way in which cities would suddenly pop up in the middle of nowhere. Clearly, there is quite a bit of building activity; I saw multiple skyscrapers, each with a construction crane sitting on top. From a contrarian perspective, I wondered at what point it might be interesting to sell short the crane operators – but perhaps the music might play for a while yet (see our recent letter, Ghost Town).

There is no stopping the music in Shanghai. By the time I arrived from my last train adventure (another urban subway after departing the bullet train) the sun was setting, triggering festive lights everywhere. At night it seems to be the custom for most of the buildings to be colourfully lit, often in apparently competitive and ostentatious displays. Even many of the ships and commuter taxis on the river were lit up, sometimes with moving animated displays. I felt as if I had entered a video game and fell asleep with visions of train tracks beneath my eyelids.

During the next day, a free Sunday before I headed in to the office, I became more familiar with the gigantic local subway system. Shanghai New International Expo Centre (17 enormous hanger-like buildings) was hosting an annual music conference, then lunch, shopping and sightseeing through Yuyuan Garden and a stroll along the Bund, old buildings on one side of the river, with the impressive Pudong skyline on the other. As my legs grew tired, I came upon an interesting sign to a strange underground crossing which promised to return me to the hotel-side of the river. I found myself sitting in a small futuristic pod vehicle crawling along through a tunnel under the river. It was as slow as the bullet train had been fast, a Disney theme-park ride with flashing lights on the tunnel walls and strange sounds. I would recommend it if you are not in a hurry and want a bit of a chuckle. My next form of transport was an ultrafast elevator. When I stepped off, I was more than 90 stories in the sky, walking along the observation deck of the Shanghai World Finance Centre. I probably spent an hour in the observation tower walking in circles, cross-referencing my map with the sights,

Another day riding along

plotting out the subway lines across the city laid out before me.

Next morning I pretended to be a local commuter on my way to work. Actually, there was no pretending. I still clearly did not fit in as I pinballed my way through the excessive crowds in the hot and stuffy tunnels. Luckily for me, a couple of generous people helped me again when I got confused at the ticketing machine. In Shanghai everyone seems to line up in orderly fashion at the designated spaces. Monitors showing arriving trains are correct and unvandalized. When the train arrives and the doors open, however, mayhem breaks loose as people shove their way in against the exiting passengers. In San Francisco it seems to be just the opposite, with no order in advance, yet when the doors open people typically let everyone out first before entering. I soon found myself adapting to the local customs lest I be left behind. Now, if I can just work on my language skills a bit more . . .

A Letter From China
17 June 2014
Geoffrey Moore

Chapter 50

False accounting

A state-owned enterprise is recruiting a chief financial officer; after several rounds of tests and interviews there are three candidates for the final interview. The company president has only one question: what is one plus one? The first candidate answers "two" and is shown the door. The second answers "three" and, with a sad smile, he too is declined. The third whispers his answer – "Whatever you want it to be" – and is hired immediately.

It is an old joke in China, but its persistence reflects the nightmare which investors here have with false accounting. Accounting is a kind of language with which investors tend not to be conversant; most of the time, investors rely on the system of company, auditor, supervisor to translate for them. How robust is the system?

I think most companies around the world have the incentive to manipulate financial reports for economic gain. In China, state-owned enterprises play an important role in the market, so there are political incentives as well. If we only talk about economic interest, to cheat or not depends on the "cost-revenue analysis": the revenue is fairly obvious, but the cost depends on whether it is easy to be caught and how serious the punishment would be. There is no global standard for supervision and punishment, and the Chinese market previously has levied a relatively low cheating cost. Even though I think auditors are stronger and more professional than before, one still needs to be careful, for the following reasons:

1. Chinese accounting principles were developed under the planned economy, not a market-oriented one. For example, revenue recognition and costing could previously be based on plans rather than the actual outcome, and bad-debt provision is still manipulated to smooth certain accounting periods' profits and losses.

2. Punishment is not harsh enough to make the cheating cost high. Recently, the China Securities Regulatory Commission reported that a listing company overstated five years of financial statements, but its punishment was only a Rmb500,000 fine.

3. In some cases, the audit processes of purportedly reputable firms may be called into question, and without the ability to fully review or consider their documentation; witness the high-profile and ongoing struggle between the Chinese-based affiliates of the "big four" US accounting firms and the US regulators seeking to compel disclosure of information.

Political interests are proving more difficult to control than economic ones. A state-owned company's president and CEO are also government officials, and any state-owned firm operates within a tangle of government interests. Officials' interests lie mainly in political promotion; promotion, of course, needs performance. Recently we have seen the reform of the state-owned sector rise towards the top of the agenda. If the sector's managers/officials gradually obtain shares in the companies they manage, their economic interests should become better aligned with those of the investor. In the short term, however, the managers of state-owned firms may manipulate the performance of their companies or falsify their accounts in order to acquire their stakes at a "comfortable" price.

The task is therefore to learn Accountingese. Even if you are not a fluent speaker, it will help you to raise necessary questions:

- Compare the company with industry peers;

- Examine the firm's performance over the past three years;

- Check the cashflow statement; people often pay attention to the balance sheet and profit-and-loss statement, but skip over the cashflow statement, which can help you cross-check;

- Avoid companies that change CFO or where the CFO resigns;

- Avoid companies that change auditor, or where the auditor resigns – unless the SEC decides to stop companies in China using the "big four" accounting firms, of course!

Site visits can help highlight possible accounting anomalies

It is always great to visit the company on site if you can. Talking to the management face to face is vital, because it is so much harder to pick up clues from documents.

The company in the picture claimed big sales for its products, but when we visited the site, inventories were piled up in the warehouse and security was poor. During our three-hour visit, we noted only two small vans loading products for delivery. Such on-site signs provide a clear warning that the facts may differ from what the company claims.

Company A:	2013	2012
Balance Sheet		
Cash and Bank	7,095,287	1,457,982
Accounts Receivable	22,306,987	1,188,192
Current Assets in Total	35,967,834	7,416,465
Non Current Assets in Total	2,052,584	879,845
P/L		
Sales	31,762,721	5,280,981
Gross Margin	88%	60%
Sales expenses	1,517,964	1,763,756
G&A	2,069,980	1,574,310
Net profit (loss)	18,354,766	(2,768,984)
Cashflow		
Net operating cash inflow	2,003,499	3,394,279

Overstating sales is the most common practice in false accounting. It is nice for sales to grow, but you should always be cautious when you note that a company's accounts receivable increase greatly in the wake of sales growth. Investors are not auditors; you cannot check the company's sales contracts or invoices. But at least you can compare figures with those of competitors and with those of the company itself in previous years, to understand whether the sales increase is an industry trend or not, and to see whether the gross margin is reasonable. You can look through the cashflow statement to check whether the accounts receivable are collected or not; if you note bad cash inflow, it is nearly always a sign that sales are being overstated. And if the company uses a non-reputable auditor, it is wise to walk away. Let's look at an example:

Company A's business increased significantly in 2013, as its new products were popular in the market, according to the management's explanation. You can see that its sales rocketed, with a sharp increase in gross margin, and the bottom line turned from a loss in 2012 to a nice gain in 2013. What a great turnaround in performance!

But you should also notice that accounts receivable increased significantly in the balance sheet, while sales expenses decreased from the previous year. This doesn't look plausible in a big year for sales. Is the increase in gross margin reasonable? Can we find comparable products in the market? When you look at the cashflow statement, you find that net operating cashflow actually decreased a lot from last year, which is abnormal.

All the above should warn you that company A might be manipulating sales for some purpose. Be careful.

Easy to catch company A? Let's take a look at company B:

Company B (in millions):	2012	2011
Balance Sheet		
Cash and Bank	260,395	388,667
Accounts Receivables	16,358	36,993
Current Assets in Total	553,139	793,588
Fixed Assets	147,740	142,300
Construction in process	188,848	86,750
Non Current Assets in Total	367,082	259,468
P/L		
Sales	269,905	232,215
Gross Margin	20%	21%
Net profit (loss)	26,553	31,179
Cashflow		
Net operating cash inflow	27,533	33,404
Net Investment cash inflow	(136,159)	(66,380)

Company B listed in 2011. Even though the industry was under pressure from 2010, the company has managed to maintain 27% sales growth in 2011 and 16% in 2012, with the gross margin stable at 20% – higher than the industry average of 12%. So, even though the net profit decreased a bit from last year, it still outperformed its industry. Accounts receivable were low, the net operating cash inflow looks reasonable with business performance; it should be fine ... shouldn't it?

Remember: overstatements of sales will result in the overstatement of an asset. Accounts receivable could be disguised as another kind of asset and would be very hard to audit if this is fixed assets or construction in process (in this case it is construction in process). You can also note that net investment cash outflow is significant, resulting in a deterioration in free cashflow.

The fact is that company B forged its sales completely, starting from 2008, in order to achieve a successful IPO in 2011. The firm used a wide range of methods to maintain its performance. It invented customers and faked sales contracts. As it "collected" accounts receivable, the company paid the money out later for "construction in process" with the ostensible purpose of expanding its business.

This doesn't mean that all financial statements that look similar to those of company A or B are definitely false, but it is certainly worth some additional digging to find out why things look as they do. Investors who fail to do so are taking a massive risk.

Construction in progress

A Letter From China
18 June 2014
Jason Xu

Chapter 51

Interesting things to do with skyscrapers

Much work has been done on Shanghai's architecture during the 1920s & 30s. I refer interested readers to the beautifully illustrated work of Tess Johnston. Less has been written on the boom in skyscraper building that we have seen over the past 25 years. The vast creation of private wealth here, combined with a government willing and able to make grand architectural statements, has led to a sustained exuberance in the design of tall buildings.

It all started here. This unlovely building, the *Shanghai Union Friendship Tower*, was the first skyscraper of the modern era, completed in 1985, just off the Bund. (The more imaginative building in the background with the leaf crown is the Bund Centre, built in 2002.) Before then, Lazlo Hudec's *Park Hotel*, alongside Shanghai's race track, had held the title of the city's tallest building since its construction in 1934. It was from this vantage point that your correspondent watched President Reagan's motorcade when he visited Shanghai in April 1984. That's the Park Hotel to the left (page 275), its 22 floors now overborne by the 47-floor Radisson New World (2005), with its "the Martians have landed" motif.

This is a late example of the revolving-restaurant fad. In the West, revolving restaurants were a thing of the 1960s and 1970s. But at that time China was busy with its own Cultural Revolution. So the 1980s was

China's first chance to build something so cool. The best example is in Shanghai's most iconic, and still rather shocking, building, the Oriental Pearl TV tower. The purple and orange velour of its revolving restaurant deserves a preservation order as a perfect period piece.

The Oriental Pearl, which held the "tallest in Shanghai" crown from 1995 to 2007, also illustrates Shanghai developers' love of coloured mirror glass – red in this case, but also popular in green and blue. Your correspondent's office from 1997 to 2005 was in the ugly *China Merchants Tower* (1995), shown below, when it enjoyed a river view which has now been entirely lost.

The last flowering of the "coloured-glass era", which mercifully now seems to be behind us, was the *Aurora Building* (2003). With its shining gold façade, this is Shanghai's "blingiest" skyscraper. What is not evident from the photograph is that the whole frontage lights up at night as a TV panel. To accommodate this, despite the fact that the building has the best view in Shanghai across the river to the Bund, the windows are only half height.

Union Friendship Tower   Radisson New World   China Merchants Tower   Aurora Building

Plaza 66, Shanghai Exhibition Centre and Portman

Once in passing I saw that the building was showing a public-services ad on the dangers of global warming! This building alone must have counted for several kilometres off the artic icepack. Aurora is a Taiwan-listed company (office furniture). This building is not included among the assets of the listed company, but is owned by the chairman. It is a shame that the building was not built to its original plan, which I once saw in Chairman Chen's office. In this model, the subsidiary building, which now hosts a fine personal art museum, was in the shape of a large golden egg! Your correspondent's office is now in the more sensible Citigroup Tower, to the right of the Aurora.

Another fad in the mid-00s was for "light boxes" – large structures stuck on top of tall buildings with no other use than to light up at night. The most notable of these are the twin towers of Grand Gateway (2005) in Xujiahui and Hang Lung's *Plaza 66*, a high-end mall on Nanjing East Road where lots of famous international brands have beautiful shops uncluttered by customers. Here *Plaza 66* rises behind the fanciful Shanghai Exhibition Centre, Stalin's gift to the Chinese people in 1955. In the background is the Portman (1990), the first modern luxury hotel complex to be completed. A modern development of the light box is the implanted LED screen, of which I am not a fan, both on artistic and environmental grounds. Every day on my way to the office I must pass

Jackie Chan extolling the virtues of Taiping Insurance on a 15-second loop.

Often the more sensible (i.e. dull) skyscrapers are the work of Hong Kong or Singaporean developers. SHK's *IFC towers* (2009/10) are a prime example. A couple of corners at higher levels have been shaved in a token "look, I'm not an oblong" way. Below it is shown with its more interesting neighbour in the background. I much prefer the building pictured on the right, *Haitong Securities Tower,* which has come up with a prettier way of disguising an essentially rectangular structure.

Another bête noir is the tendency of Chinese architects to pastiche; the weird and wonderful *Moller House,* built for the eponymous Swedish shipping tycoon in 1936, deserves better than the horrible Chinese apartment blocks that now surround it. The architect behind the new *Ping An* building also got rather carried away with his Greek columns (all Ionic).

There's nothing token about the phallic *Tomorrow's Square* (2003). It

IFC towers   Haitong Securities   Moller House

looks as though it hosts one of the rocket-killing laser guns favoured by James Bond villains. The central pearl had been temporarily turned into a football in honour of the World Cup. *Bocom Financial Tower* is the one that Tom Cruise slid down in Mission Impossible III when attacking a group of Chinese baddies. In the lobby it says that these floors are occupied by the offices of China Pacific Insurance, but we know better.

Feng shui is an important feature in skyscraper design here, and this has resulted in a number of buildings with holes in the middle (to let through the qi, don't you know). The *Shanghai Stock Exchange Building* (1997) has a hole in the middle of it (no jokes please). The impact of this rather impressive building has, however, been masked now by the less interesting skyscrapers subsequently built around it. The feng shui of atriums would occupy a complete additional letter, but I show the photo (page 279 top right) as it combines so many elements. It is symmetrical with two imperial lions either side of the door. There is also water, a regular feature in Chinese atria, though given Shanghai's relatively high rainfall, one would have thought that the architects might like to concentrate on keeping the water out. Often the stone ball supported by water pressure has stopped working, so kudos to Pudong Development Bank for keeping this ball rolling.

Ping An

Tomorrow's Square

Bocom Financial Tower

Size matters. Despite the lessons of 9/11, developers still appear to want to achieve the biggest erection. There are a variety of rooftop constructions; I rather like the simple but elegant twisting bands on top of the *Jing An China Tower Building* (1988), behind the extravagant temple of the same

Pudong Development Bank atrium

name. The simplest way to increase the size, however, while saving a little money, is to cheat and put a large pylon on top of your skyscraper. In the *Shimao Internatonal Plaza* (2006) the architect has splashed out and gone for two, in a sort of rugby-post style.

Most guilty, in this regard, however, is Dubai's Burj Khalifa, which is the world's tallest building, courtesy of its pylon, while our Shanghai World Finance Centre actually has the highest occupied floor. SWFC had a somewhat troubled gestation. The site, a driving range, was dug up in 1997, just before the Asian Financial Crisis. It remained a large hole in the ground for a number of years. After work was re-started, the original design, with a circle at the top, was rejected as looking too much like the Japanese flag (a sensitive subject, as the developer was Mori). Completed in its new approved form in 2008, it is referred to as the "bottle opener". The glass-floored observation deck on the 100th floor is not recommended to vertigo sufferers.

Jing An China Tower   **White Magnolia**

The skyline continues to change each year. The SWFC surpassed the interesting Jinmao Tower, which is all about the power of eight (88 floors, opened on 28/8/08). This most "Chinese" of skyscrapers was actually designed by Skidmore, Owings & Merrill of Chicago, and has proved a magnet for illegal climbers and base jumpers. Now SWFC is to be surpassed in its turn by the government-financed, 632-metre, 121-floor monster known simply as Shanghai Tower. The design, like a rolled-up newspaper, features a novel double-layer façade, and the tower will be serviced by 106 elevators. It has already topped out and should be ready for occupation next year. Let's hope Shanghai avoids the curse of the tallest tower. As the Shanghai market is already down nearly 70% from its peak in 2007, completion seems rather belated.

Shimao International Plaza

Shanghai is not ideal terrain for skyscraper building. Piles need to be sunk more than 80 metres into the Shanghai mud to support the tallest buildings. The story about Shanghai gradually sinking under the weight is a regular filler for local newspapers in the silly season. But still from my window I can see cranes working on exciting new projects. The one below, built on a record-breakingly expensive plot of land on the river bank, is to be called White Magnolia Plaza. There is talk of a

838m Sky City in Changsha, and a design for a pair of towers both 1 km high, called the Phoenix Nest, has been approved in Wuhan. But these remain pie in the sky. In Shanghai, the dreams are already solidified in concrete, steel and glass.

For readers who would like an exhaustive and illustrated list of Shanghai's skyscrapers (or to see what White Magnolia Plaza will look like) please see the niche website www.skyscraperpage.com.

the Big 3

A Letter From China
21 July 2014
Chris Ruffle

About the authors

CHRIS RUFFLE

Fluent in Mandarin, Chris has been based in the Far East since 1983. He initially worked in Beijing, Shanghai and Australia for Wogen Resources. He moved to Tokyo in 1987 as analyst for Warburg Securities and established the firm's Taiwan office in 1990. Chris joined Martin Currie in 1994, moving to work in Taipei from 2000 and Shanghai from 2002. Chris left Martin Currie in 2006 with colleague Ke Shifeng to form MC China Ltd, buying out the joint venture in 2011 and establishing the Open Door Capital Group, a fund management company dedicated to specialist China strategies.

(Chapters 3, 12. 16, 28-31, 33-36, 39, 42, 44-45, 51)

JUSTIN CROZIER

Justin joined Open Door as head of communications from Martin Currie Investment Management, where he led the investment-writing team. Before joining Martin Currie in 2006, he worked for Harper Collins Publishers, where he was an editor for Collins Dictionaries with responsibility for PR. From 1998 to 2002, he lived in Beijing, where he taught English at Beijing Language & Culture University. Justin read history at the University of Oxford, where he also took a master's degree in Byzantine studies. He returned to the UK in 2013 and is now a senior writer with Copylab. He continues to work on Open Door's communications and returns to China regularly.

(Chapters 1, 4-11, 13-15, 17-27, 32)

WU BIN (TONY WU), CFA

Tony started his investment career in 1993 as an assistant analyst with Peregrine Brokerage. From 1996 to 1999 he worked as an analyst for Heartland Capital Investment Consulting, Martin Currie's joint venture with China Securities. During this time, he built an extensive knowledge of China's industries and equity markets, and gained valuable insights into how Chinese companies operate. He left to co-found a private investment consulting business in Shanghai. Tony returned to Heartland Capital Investment Consulting in September 2004 as a senior analyst and became head of research in 2012.

(Chapter 37)

YANG LIQIN (REBECCA YANG)

Rebecca worked for Heartland Capital Investment Consulting from 2003 to 2014 as an investment analyst. Previously, she worked for British American Tobacco China, where she was responsible for the marketing and financial management of its offices in two provinces. She has an MBA from Edinburgh University.

(Chapter 2)

LIN YUEHUA (WARREN LIN)

Warren joined Heartland Capital Investment Consulting in 2007 as an investment analyst. Before that he worked for eight years at Fubon Investment Trust, the largest active-investment house in Taiwan, first as an analyst and later as a fund manager. Warren has an MBA from National Taipei University and is fluent in Mandarin and English.

(Chapters 41, 43)

WANG ZHUFENG (JOE WANG)

Joe joined Heartland Capital Investment Consulting in 2010 as an investment analyst. He came to the company from Japan Invest Group, where he was a senior equity analyst covering the Chinese property sector. Before that, he spent three years as an analyst at Evolution Securities Group. Between 1995 and 2003, Joe held a variety of roles, including financial controller, with China Resources (Holding) Corporation in Hong Kong. He began his career at the Ministry of Foreign Trade and Investment in Beijing in 1994. He has an MBA and is a certified public accountant in China.

(Chapter 47)

XU BIN (JASON XU)

Jason joined Heartland Capital Investment Consulting as a due-diligence analyst in 2010. He came to the company from Car Val Investors, where he was senior acquisition analyst. Before that, he worked for GEM Services as a corporate audit manager and, earlier, for Intel Technology in Singapore, where he was responsible for financing and risk management in the company's Asia Pacific distribution system. He began his career as an auditor at Ernst & Young in 2001.

(Chapters 38, 50)

CHEN YUN (VICKY CHEN)

Vicky Chen joined Heartland's Shanghai-based team in 2008 as a partner in the China Healthcare Partnership. She arrived at Heartland after four years as a China healthcare/life sciences analyst at UBS Warburg, during which time she was ranked the number-one health care analyst for Asia ex-Japan in the Institutional Investor Survey and Extel Survey 2007. Vicky has over a decade's experience as a healthcare specialist, having worked variously in consulting, marketing, project management and R&D. Vicky was born in Shanghai but trained in the US. She now acts as a consultant to Open Door.

(Chapter 40)

GEOFFREY MOORE

Geoff joined the Open Door team in 2013 after two decades of managing legal and regulatory initiatives at highly regarded brokerage and advisory firms, as well as at small start-up investment companies. At Wells Capital Management, Geoff managed compliance, liquidity and credit risk matters on behalf of separately managed accounts and money-market mutual funds. Before joining Wells Fargo, he represented Charles Schwab and Co., Inc. as corporate counsel on a variety of broker-dealer and securities-market issues, including litigation and arbitration matters, corporate finance and structured-products transactions, capital markets and syndicate issues. Geoff received his JD in 1994 from the University of California, Hastings College of the Law, and is a member of the California State Bar. He received a BS in Economics and a BA in Music from Wesleyan University in 1990.

(Chapters 48, 49)